VISION
INVESTING

VISION INVESTING

HOW WE BEAT WALL STREET & YOU CAN, TOO!

EUGENE NG

The fundamental concept is that you should not rely upon the information or opinions you read. Rather, you should use what you read here as starting points for doing independent research on companies and investing techniques, then judge for yourself the merits of the material that has been shared.

We do not guarantee the veracity, reliability or completeness of any information provided. You are responsible for your own investment decisions. We will not be responsible for any errors or omissions in articles or postings, for hyperlinks embedded in messages, or for any results obtained from the use of such information. We will not be liable for any loss or damage caused by a reader's reliance on this information. If you don't accept this responsibility for yourself, you should not continue reading further.

In the material and data that we make available in this book, we rely on a wide variety of sources, such as YCharts and the Internet. We believe these sources of data to be accurate and reliable, but sometimes they may not be. We make no claims or representations as to the accuracy, completeness, or truth of any material contained in our areas. Nor are we liable for any errors in the data. We promise not to lie to you, but we reserve the right to be wrong.

To my mother and wife,
Mary and Mag

Thank you for supporting me
and being here for me always.

"Never forget who was there for you, when no one else was."

Quotes that inspired me to write this book:

"Make your portfolio reflect your best vision for our future".
- David Gardner

"Always be thinking ahead, be optimistic,
think about the world that you want to create.
Because sure enough, your dollars and mine, our
capital is helping shape the world.
Truly we are shaping the world every day with our financial decisions."
- David Gardner

"Timing the market is a fool's game.
Whereas **time in the market is your greatest advantage.**"
- Nick Murray

"In the short-term, the market goes down faster than it goes up.
But over the long-term, the market goes up
more eventually than it goes down.
The long run is the only term that counts."
- David Gardner

"I find excellence, buy excellence, and add to excellence over time.
I sell mediocrity. That's how I invest."
- David Gardner

"Investing in great companies early in their high growth stages, that are
the most innovative and forward-thinking,
then holding them for the long term,
will provide the highest possible returns."
- David Gardner

"Going where other investors won't.
Doing what other investors don't"
- David Gardner

CONTENTS

PART III
THE LONG-TERM VIEW & MINDSET

FOREWORD

Thousands of books have been written about investing. This is a very personal book to me, as it is my first ever to be completed and within a very short span of less than a month. It will be biased, probably has huge gaps, and of course, it is far too short. But then, it is really a start in this journey of investing for me and hopefully for you as well.

Our investing beliefs have been shaped by the media. The message we are fed is that only a handful of great investors can beat the market and have managed to outperform the markets consistently, therefore, we should just invest in the market via low-cost ETFs (and just be as average as the market) or maybe invest in some of these great investor's funds. There is probably some truth to it, which we will cover in greater detail, but for me, everything in nature is statistics and a bell curve. There will always be the tail end or right side of the curve where there are people who will do very well, and the left side of the curve where others will do very badly. The majority of which will either slightly outperform or underperform.

I, along with many investors today, stand on the shoulders of these great investors, wanting to be like them. Investing started off being a personal lifelong quest for me. I am probably similar to you. In my early days, I "bought and invested" in stocks only to lose money. I became terrified and maybe even stopped investing as a result. Because of this, it became my quest to find my guru in investing, learn from the best out there, and master investing. For me, it is and will be a lifelong journey. Let me share a little bit more about my journey...

What having no or little money teaches you...

I was very fortunate to be born and raised in Singapore (in Asia) with a younger brother to two lovely middle-income parents. In my early teenage years, life was not the easiest. My father was a habitual gambler and soon left my mother with huge gambling debts to repay. My parents divorced not long after. My mother took over sole custody of the children and had to scrimp and save every single dollar over many years to repay all the monies to all her loving relatives and friends whom she had borrowed from. The value of money and the management of it was extremely important to me as a belief, and I never wanted my mother to go through that again. She went through so much to bring both of us single-handedly.

My life story was deeply influenced and impacted by the following two life incidents which also shaped how I think about things.

What sports teach you...

I was a national sportsman and athlete in my younger adult days, where I represented the Singapore National Team in the 2007 Southeast Asian (SEA) Games and won our 22nd consecutive water polo team gold for the country. Representing Singapore and winning was one of the highest responsibilities and things that I could do for my nation. For those who have not heard of water polo, think of it as underwater wrestling combined with soccer in a swimming pool with 13 players in each team, but 7 players playing at any one time, including the goalkeeper, with unlimited substitutions.

But what you did not know was that I was probably one of the oldest to have ever made the cut for my first SEA Games, and I was also the last player of thirteen players to be picked. Simply put, I was never the most talented, the smartest, the strongest, the biggest, the tallest, nor the fastest player in the team. But I made up for it in pure dedication, commitment, and hard work. In the two earlier games held in 2003 and 2005 held bi-annually, I was not even remotely close to making the shortlist, much less being considered. Then came 2006, where I made a personal declaration and decision that I would drastically change my mentality and to give it my final shot at making the team. By this time, I had been playing the sport for more than 12 years and more than 8 years at the youth and national team level.

It suddenly dawned upon me that I was doing this wrong all this while and had been training "blindly." As Bruce Lee says, "I fear not the man who has practiced 10,000 kicks once, but I fear the man who has practiced one kick 10,000 times." I was the guy who practiced 10,000 kicks once, not the latter. I decided to do things differently by spending 1 hour or more before and after every training and game visualizing all the plays, correcting my errors, what I did well, and letting it all play out in my head. Slowly but surely, my performance in the pool improved. The main takeaways from this experience are "**You need to commit to being great at whatever you do. When you focus on it hard enough, with relentless passion, commitment, and dedication, you can make absolutely anything happen. Nothing is impossible. We can be the best at what we want to be.**" It is with this **drive, determination, and positivity** that are the anchor points in my life and in everything that I do.

What being foolish and stupid teaches you...

Christmas of 2015, this young and brash kid was clearly having too many drinks at a beach club with a shallow swimming pool. He decided to do the most foolish thing ever: a somersault into the pool. I subsequently **broke my neck with a Jefferson C1 burst fracture** where my first cervical collar bone shattered into two pieces. I underwent a surgical operation to put on a halo-vest, a metal structure to hold my neck in place with four screws into my skull for almost three months. That began my painful phase to recovery. What I didn't understand at the time was **how lucky I was to not only survive but to not be paralyzed**. My doctor said to me, "Eugene, you are so lucky to have survived. Most people who have this injury have died, and if they did not die, they would have likely been paralyzed." Upon realizing how blessed I was to still be alive and have recovered (not fully, one part of the fracture healed, the other leaving a 5mm open gap still), it was then I decided that **happiness and quality time with my loved ones**

is very important and dear to me. With the remaining time I had in my life, I needed to make the most out of it and do something for myself, my loved ones, and other people. In addition, I learned **how to be grateful for the life we have and to show gratitude every day**.

"You can't do anything about the length of your life,
*but **you can do something about its width and its depth**."*
- Shira Tehran

"The two most important days of your life are the day you were born,
*and **the day you find out why**."*
- Mark Twain

*"There are **only two ways to live your life**:*
one is as if everything is a miracle,
*the other **is as though nothing is a miracle**."*
- Albert Einstein

Why investing then...

After this incident, I made a conscious decision that I wanted to manage my money properly and grow my wealth. I knew **investing was one of the three pillars to building and growing wealth** (as that's how most rich people do), the other two being properties and owning a business. I focused on investing first because it was something I could do from anywhere in the world from the comfort of my iPad.

I needed to master investing. But before that, I needed to find and learn from the best. I had been reading about Warren Buffett by then and a number of his teachings resonated with me.

Why the mindset is so important...

By chance (thank you Facebook), I stumbled upon Ken Chee who ran the Millionaire Investor Program (MIP) and paid a fortune to join his 3-day value investing course back then. Ken imparted life-changing wisdom: **be**

greedy when others are fearful. That **changed my mindset to market sell-offs, which I now look forward to as massive buying opportunities**. Fear somewhat disappeared from how I looked at things. However, the approach they were advocating—buying solid and boring businesses and buying great companies at cheap prices, was not working out for me.

Why value investing was not working out for me...

At the time, some of these companies typically had a moat or competitive advantage and they were the leader in monopolies, duopolies, oligopolies in the business they were in. But often, the addressable market itself matured and growth slowed down or even contracted for some. If earnings grew single digits between 0-5%, it would almost be impossible for the stock price to increase more than 10-15% in any given year unless the business significantly changed or pivoted. If revenues grow at low single digits or eventually stagnate or even decline, it is extremely difficult for a company to continuously grow profits faster than revenues. That would indefinitely increase profit margins. Not to say it's not impossible, but it is extremely rare to find in reality. And when earnings stop growing as fast or even decline, the company's share price eventually just follows lower as well.

And in the latter, we used complicated discounted cash flow models, basically excel spreadsheets with a large number of assumptions about future growth, which in my opinion was nothing more than touching my finger to the sky. Garbage in, garbage out. No one can predict with 100% certainty as to what the company would do in 5 years' time. Can you find me an equity research analyst who can do that year after year, quarter after quarter whose price targets were the same as the eventual stock price? The answer is a resounding *no*.

The bigger instructive lesson was that based on traditional valuation metrics and the safety of margin, one would never buy any of these stocks and miss out on investing in some of the bigger multibaggers. Mind you, investor optimism does not continue to push a stock price on an upward path of 5, 10, 15, 20 years beating the market. It might be crazy speculation in the near term for minutes, hours, days, maybe months, but not years.

One of my favorite quotes by Benjamin Graham which greatly shapes how I think about the markets in the short-term (which is 100% noise), is this:

"In the **short run**, the market is a **voting machine**
but in the **long run**, the market is a **weighing machine**."
- Benjamin Graham

There was something else, and that was what Value Investing was missing for me.

I set my screens and investment criteria and searched across more than 10,000 listed companies globally available for me to invest in, and I struggled to find any company with more than 10% growth rates that fit the criteria I was looking for. I also realized that Berkshire Hathaway (run by Warren Buffett and Charlie Munger) was effectively behaving like the S&P 500 and no longer outperformed as it used to at least since the 2008 financial crisis. My hypothesis is that (1) Berkshire Hathaway has gotten so large that they are struggling to deploy capital meaningful enough to account for decent returns (2) the cash float resulting in a drag on return on capital and (3) they end up buying good but struggling businesses with a large safety of margin and continued to struggle.

Berkshire Hathaway versus the S&P 500 (since 2009)

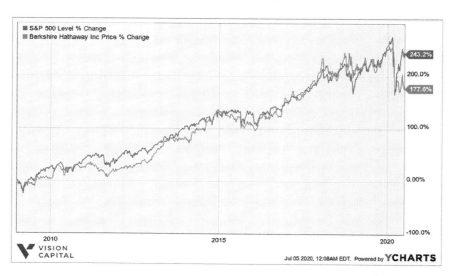

Berkshire Hathaway versus the S&P 500 (5-year chart)

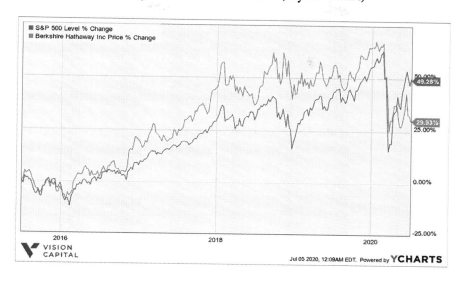

Berkshire Hathaway versus the S&P 500 (3-year chart)

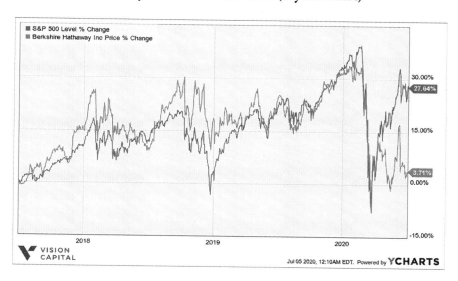

That was the awakening moment for me...

An Investor's Search to Be a Fool...

In my search globally, **I was not able to find an investor's approach that would resonate with me and made sense.** Yes, I understood Value Investing and its math of buying great businesses and even better prices which provides a margin of safety, therefore lowering downside risk and hopefully providing more upside. But I could only see myself holding some of these businesses for the next 3-5 years and they *could* struggle. What happened to long-term investing? Thus, **I needed to find and create an investing framework that was better suited to me** and yet **everlasting enough to continue for many more years to come.**

I came across **The Motley Fool** and the **two brothers, David and Tom Gardner,** and I was especially intrigued by their investing philosophy. When I saw the following charts their investing recommendation service, **Stock Advisor, returning 392%** beating the market single-handedly, I immediately jumped on board their stock picking service and signed up over three years ago—Stock Advisor, Rule Breakers and the whole breadth of services. You will also find that a large part of how I think with respect to investing is significantly influenced by The Motley Fool, Tom and David Gardner, and many other investing legends including Peter Lynch, Warren Buffett, Charlie Munger, and Franklin Templeton.

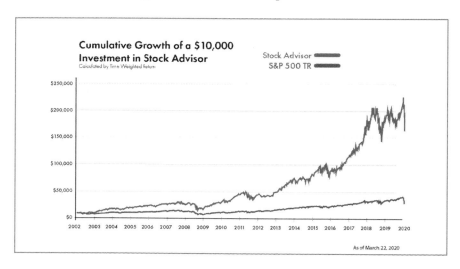

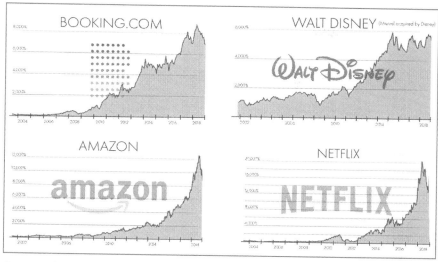

Source: The Motley Fool (as of 31 March 2020)

Co-Founders of The Motley Fool, Tom and David Gardner

Source: The Motley Fool

If you want a stock-picking service, trust me there is nothing better than The Motley Fool (which I highly recommend), but I'm not suggesting you put this book away and go and join them right away.

More importantly, what I want you to understand is that **I do not believe in giving you the fish. Instead, I believe not just in giving you the fishing rod, but in the process, teaching you how to fish and fish for the big catch.** You can continue adjusting your techniques to catch other bigger fishes in time to come.

Because even if you are provided with the 50 best-performing stocks for the next 5 years, what would you do with it? When the market doubles, would you rush to sell everything? You probably would ask yourself, why not? When the market sells down 40%, would you say this is crap and sell off everything? Or would you not buy because you hear from someone saying that it is overvalued and it is expensive, only to realize the stock price doubled not long after?

And that is really what I wish to pass to you in this book. It is a combination of everything that I have learned, found useful, and what I practice day in day out of my investment journey. Investing is also what I can do for the rest of my life. **Investing is my Ikigai,** my reason for being: **What I love, What I am good at, What the world needs, and What I can be paid for.** You will find that I aim to teach you something not just about investing, but also about life. Hopefully, you learn something out of it.

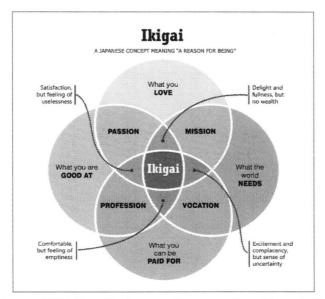

Source: IKIGAI — The Japanese Secret to a Long Happy Life by Hector Garcia and Francesc Miralles.

When you find your life's purpose and mission...

*"When **you love people** and **have the desire to make a profound, positive impact upon the world**, then will you have **accomplished the meaning to live.**"*
- Sasha Azevedo

There was a year-long search for my own Life Mission which culminated in the below:

*"**My Life Mission is to excite, inspire, and empower people to pursue their dreams and to grow their business to create long term sustainable positive value by making the world and mankind a better future.**"*
- Eugene Ng

Hence, Vision Investing, my style of investing. This is my Investing Mission:

"To make our portfolio reflect our vision of our future."
- David Gardner

Vision Capital, which is the investment fund I currently run with all of my own capital, **aims solely to invest in companies that are changing and shaping the world for the better.**

I hope you will truly be inspired by my book, that it will resonate with you, and you will adopt a variation whether in part or in whole of my approach.

I **truly believe everyone** (YES! Including YOU!) **can be an investor and outperform and beat the market.** We have all the advantages that Wall Street does not have. But first, we need to change our beliefs, right our mindset, and have the tools to think correctly about investing. Enjoy! I hope in the process we can make you become smarter, happier, and richer.

I will leave you with a temporary parting quote...

The True Joy of Life...

*"This is the **true joy in life, being used for a purpose recognized by yourself as a mighty one. Being a force of nature** instead of a feverish, selfish little clod of ailments and grievances, complaining that the world will not devote itself to making you happy. I am of the opinion that **my life belongs to the whole community and as long as I live**, it is **my privilege to do for it what I can. I want to be thoroughly used up when I die, for the harder I work, the more I live. I rejoice in life for its own sake.** Life is no brief candle to me. It is a sort of **splendid torch** which I have got hold of for the moment and I want to **make it burn as brightly as possible before handing it on to future generations."**
- George Bernard Shaw*

YOUR PREMISE AND BELIEFS WITH RESPECT TO INVESTING

Your Premise refers to the **foundational beliefs you currently hold** with respect to investing, buying equities, etc.: Your **WHATs**.

- *What do you believe? Have you made or lost money? How have you done?*
- *Are your beliefs empowering or disempowering?*
- *Do your beliefs move you at a deep level or are they holding you back?*
- *What are your beliefs for investing, or what would you like it to be?*

E.g. **My Original Premise** when I first started out:

- Investing is one of the three pillars I can build and grow my wealth.
- I have yet to outperform and beat the market, but given that there are so many investors who have done so (e.g. Warren Buffett, John Templeton, etc.) in the past, I know and believe I can be just as good, if not better than them.
- I will not just be the market average and just invest in ETFs. I want to master investing. I want to be one of the best investors in the world. I want to go on beating the market at investing for as long as I live.

What are your current Premises and Beliefs with respect to investing?

We want you to spend a couple of minutes to write yours down in the space below. Because if you know and understand yourself and where you stand, half the battle is already won.

_____

_____

_____

_____

_____

_____

_____

_____

_____

_____

_____

_____

_____

PART I
PREPARING TO INVEST

CHAPTER 1

WHY INVESTING? WHY EQUITIES?

Why Invest in Equities?

There are broadly three primary ways to build and store lasting wealth. They are:

1) **Business**
2) **Real Estate / Property** (including homes)
3) **Financial Assets** (Stocks, Bonds, Cash, etc)

The following three charts below state the clearest comparison and how the composition of a person's net worth evolves as they become wealthier. There are three main ways to build your wealth, either via (1) own **business**, (2) **property / real estate,** and (3) **investing**.

But this is not a book to teach you neither about (1) how to start or scale a profitable business or (2) buying and investing in undervalued real estate properties. There are many great books and experts from whom you can learn from out there.

Rather, we **will focus on the third way** of how the rich and the wealthy invest in their wealth. **In particular, investing, and more specifically in financial assets— specifically in equities** via **individual equities** (stocks), not mutual funds, index funds, or ETFs.

1

THE COMPOSITION OF WEALTH

The composition of household wealth tends to change a lot as people move up the economic ladder.

Most of a middle class household's wealth will be derived from their principal residence, whereas the very rich have a far higher percentage of business equity and financial assets in the mix.

100% ├─────────── 80% ─────── AMERICAN HOUSEHOLD WEALTH BRACKETS ─── 20% ─────────── 1% ┤ 0%

| LOWER INCOME | MIDDLE INCOME | UPPER INCOME | ULTRA RICH |

MIDDLE INCOME
% OF GROSS ASSETS

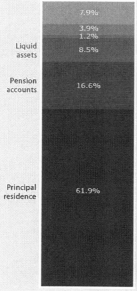

Liquid assets — 7.9% / 3.9% / 1.2% / 8.5%

Pension accounts — 16.6%

Principal residence — 61.9%

NET WORTH
$0–$471K

UPPER INCOME
% OF GROSS ASSETS

24.5%

18.6%

1.2%
7.7%

22.4%

25.6%

NET WORTH
$471K–$10.3M

THE ULTRA RICH
% OF GROSS ASSETS

Business equity and other real estate — 49.0%

Stocks, securities, mutual funds, and trusts — 31.4%

Misc. assets — 1.4% / 6.7% / 6.0% / 7.6%

NET WORTH
$10.3M+

Source: Edward N. Wolff (2017). Survey of Consumer Finances

2

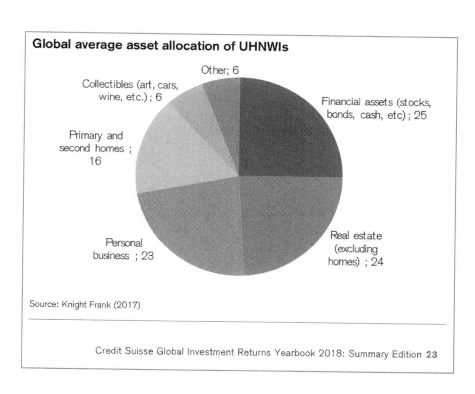

Global average asset allocation of UHNWIs

Other; 6

Collectibles (art, cars, wine, etc.) ; 6

Financial assets (stocks, bonds, cash, etc) ; 25

Primary and second homes ; 16

Personal business ; 23

Real estate (excluding homes) ; 24

Source: Knight Frank (2017)

Credit Suisse Global Investment Returns Yearbook 2018: Summary Edition **23**

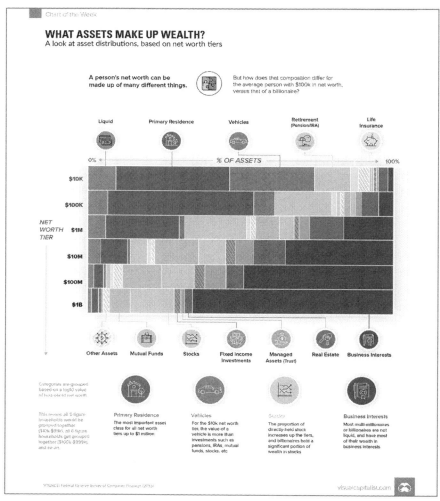

Source: Visual Capitalist
https://www.visualcapitalist.com/chart-assets-make-wealth/

Equities Are the Only Asset Class That Beats All Others

According to a Credit Suisse study[1], just looking at the US market, for example, **stocks** 9.4% p.a. (equities) **outperformed bonds** 4.9% p.a. (fixed income), **bills** 3.7% p.a. and inflation's 2.9% p.a. by a wide margin. Thus, **stocks have decisively outpaced bonds and cash**, making them the **most profitable investment over the last 120 years**. You don't need an advanced degree in finance to figure out which path wins that contest.

US Equities Trounce Bonds and Bills in Both Nominal and Real Terms

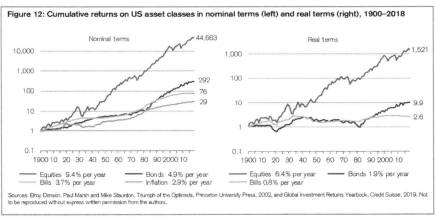

Figure 12: Cumulative returns on US asset classes in nominal terms (left) and real terms (right), 1900–2018

Source: Credit Suisse Global Investment Returns Yearbook 2019

---

[1] Source: Credit Suisse Global Investment Returns Yearbook 2019
https://www.credit-suisse.com/media/assets/corporate/docs/about-us/research/publications/csri-summary-edition-credit-suisse-global-investment-returns-yearbook-2019.pdf

Real Annualized Equity Returns Are Positive in All of the 21 Countries Tracked

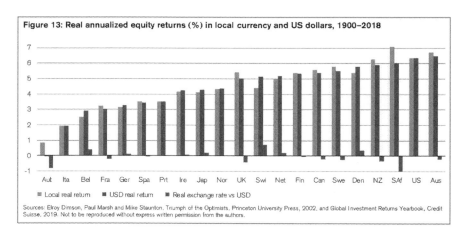

Figure 13: Real annualized equity returns (%) in local currency and US dollars, 1900–2018

Sources: Elroy Dimson, Paul Marsh and Mike Staunton, Triumph of the Optimists, Princeton University Press, 2002, and Global Investment Returns Yearbook, Credit Suisse, 2019. Not to be reproduced without express written permission from the authors.

Equities Beat All Other Assets

In a chart shared by Lauren Templeton, **stocks (9.9%) beat bonds** (6.2%), gold (5.8%), oil (5.6%), international stocks (5.0%), property (3.1%) and the **average investor (2.5%)**. Now, how is that possible if all these asset classes outperform the average investor? It's because people are really terrible decision-makers and they are often at times buying high and selling low (though they can tell you the opposite).

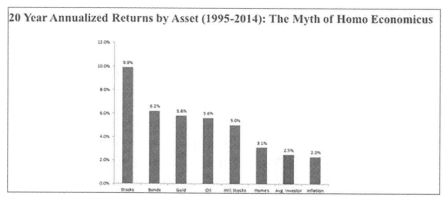

20 Year Annualized Returns by Asset (1995-2014): The Myth of Homo Economicus

Source: Lauren Templeton: *Investing the Templeton Way* [Transcript][2]

---

[2] Source: https://geoinvesting.com/investing-templeton-way-transcript/

What Are the Considerations of Investing in Equities vs Other Financial Assets?

Equities return above inflation, **have high liquidity,** one **can invest in small amounts on a regular basis,** and **can potentially be less complex.** And transactions **can be executed electronically via our mobile phones or laptop in minutes if not seconds.**

The **only consideration for investing in equities is probably the high volatility.** Unfortunately, this is **not something that we can control,** but what **we can control is how we respond, react to it,** and manage our emotions and temperament.

COMPARING VARIOUS ASSET CLASSES

Criteria	Equity	Fixed Income	Real Estate	Commodities	Cash
Return Potential	Above Inflation	Near Inflation	Above Inflation	Near Inflation	Below Inflation
Volatility in Returns	High	Low	High	High	Nil
Liquidity	Very High	High	Very Low	Low	NA
Can one invest small amounts ?	Yes	Yes	No	Sometimes	NA
Can one invest every month/year	Yes	Yes	No	No	NA
Complexity	Average	Less	High	High	NIL

www.jagoinvestor.com

7

You Are the Best Person to Manage Your Own Money

Ultimately, this is capped by the very idea that **you should manage your own money yourself.** Because **you are the individual most personally invested in your own financial success** (no one else!), you are the one best suited to make your money decisions.

Some of you at this point might want us to get straight to the point and tell you "How do I get rich?" or "What stocks to buy?". This is not that sort of book. If you are interested in fast cash, a quick search on Google reveals 1,690,000 results for "get rich." But this is not our style. We **take the long view.**

> *"Give a man a fish, and you'll feed him for a day.*
> ***Teach a man to fish, and you've fed him for a lifetime."***
> *- Confucius*

We would **rather teach you how to fish** rather give you fish. This book is written for those who understand that there is **significantly more to investing** than a studio host on CNBC or Bloomberg shouting, "Buy, Buy, Buy!" This book is for those who understand and appreciate that investing is a lifelong pursuit that (when done right) will set us up for the financial freedom and future we want. Investing is only one part of the equation, and we hope to get you thinking right about this.

In what follows, we hope **to help you and the world invest better**, giving you the **confidence and knowledge,** you need **to succeed as an individual investor.**

QUICK SUMMARY

- The rich grow their wealth via **individual equities.**
- **Stocks have outpaced bonds and cash** and have been the **most profitable investment over the last 120 years.**
- You are most invested in your success, **manage your own money!**

CHAPTER 2

WHY DO WE NOT TRADE WHEN IT COMES TO INVESTING?

Trading and investing in stocks both involve taking a position on a financial market in order **to profit from price movements**. However, they pursue this goal in **vastly different ways**.

Traders tend to trade a short-term **speculative position** on the underlying market price to profit from buying. To take advantage of price increase or vice versa, they go short if they think the price will decline.

Investors instead tend to take a longer-term look at markets, assessing the **future health and growth prospects of a company** over years and even decades, and then buy and hold them for **long-term gains**. Traders or speculators look at rising and falling markets over a **shorter-time frame** to profit from volatility.

Fact No. 1: Market predictions have been wrong far more often than right

For starters, **not a single person has accurately predicted an economic recession in almost fifty years**. They have also missed many market recoveries, including the unusually broad and global expansion of 2017.

What about well-known investment newsletter writers and strategists who claim to have tactical strategies to time the markets? They don't do any better.

In economist William Sharpe's 1975 study, "Likely Gains from Market Timing[3]", the Nobel laureate showed that **investors would need a whopping forecasting accuracy of 74%** **to outperform a diversified buy-and-hold portfolio.** Remarkably, when a study by Goh Yang Chye of GYC Financial Advisory analyzed 6,582 public forecasts that well-known experts had made from 1998 to 2012, they found that the **most accurate among them had a rate of only 68%.** This was clearly not even enough to beat the benchmark (i.e. 74%)! The **average** accuracy was a **much lower 47.4%.**

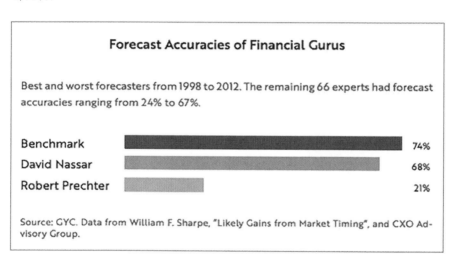

Forecast Accuracies of Financial Gurus

Best and worst forecasters from 1998 to 2012. The remaining 66 experts had forecast accuracies ranging from 24% to 67%.

Benchmark	74%
David Nassar	68%
Robert Prechter	21%

Source: GYC. Data from William F. Sharpe, "Likely Gains from Market Timing", and CXO Advisory Group.

Fact No. 2: The odds are statistically stacked against traders

It would still be erroneous to suggest that investors would never be able to beat the market with a well-established market-timing strategy. The **difficulty**, however, **is in being able to do so consistently over a period of time**. This is simply because the **mathematics of market timing is**

[3] Likely Gains from Market Timing by William F. Sharpe
Financial Analysts Journal Vol. 31, No. 2 (Mar. - Apr., 1975), pp. 60-69 https://www.jstor.org/stable/4477805?seq=1

against them from the very start. For every market-timing decision requires not just one call, but two calls: one to buy and one to sell. When timing the market, an investor has to decide not just when to sell, but also when to buy back into the market. Let's say that a spectacular new investment guru manages to consistently get a "sell" call correct 70% of the time and also a "buy" call correct 70% of the time. The probability of executing both a market exit and a re-entry at the right time then becomes **70% multiplied by 70%**, which is **49%**. Those are **worse odds than flipping a coin** (50% chance that a coin lands on heads and 50% that it falls on tails)!

What if this **strategy requires** you to **buy and sell a second time**? **Mathematically**, your **likelihood of success goes down to a dismal 24%**. If you had to string even more trades together, well...you can see where I'm going with this. The unfortunate reality is that **each subsequent trade gives you ever-decreasing odds for success**, and yet, this is something that many investors seem oblivious to.

It Gets Worse the More You Trade!

SELL Call Accuracy		BUY Call Accuracy		SELL Call Accuracy		BUY Call Accuracy		Trade Accuracy
70%	X	70%	X	70%	X	70%	=	24%

Source: GYC. Data from William F. Sharpe, "Likely Gains from Market Timing".

Fact No.3: Perfectly timing the market does not really get you a lot more

Below illustrate three siblings who started investing $10,000 a year in global stocks from 1977 for 40 years. Jane, who is the perfect market timer, invests at the market low for the year. Jack, who does not time the market, invests on the first day of each year. John, who is a poor market timer, invests at the high of each year.

Jane (perfect timing) ends up with **9.3%** p.a. annualized returns, vs **Jack's (no timing) 9.1%** p.a. and **John's (poor timing) 8.8%** p.a. The more instructive lesson comes into the end portfolio value at the end of 40 years and particularly **because of the power of compounding**. Jane (perfect timing) ends up with $4.35mil, Jack (no timing) ends up with $4.11mil but John (poor timing) ends up with much lower at $3.57mil.

The key learning from this is to ask ourselves **if we can perfectly time the markets all the time**? I definitely cannot, and most investment and trading experts who have consistently outperformed the markets over the long run do not either. Why would you want to try to do something different when the potential downside from poor market timing is far more detrimental than the potential upside from perfect market timing? This is not to say that you cannot trade (making money by timing the markets), but **separate trading from investing**.

This is also not to say that you should be 100% fully invested all the time, as we believe **having some reserve of spare cash on the sidelines** can be particularly useful in helping us manage our temperaments and how we deal with ourselves.

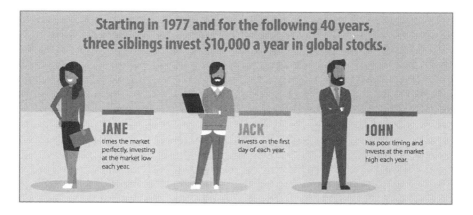

Starting in 1977 and for the following 40 years, three siblings invest $10,000 a year in global stocks.

JANE times the market perfectly, investing at the market low each year.

JACK invests on the first day of each year.

JOHN has poor timing and invests at the market high each year.

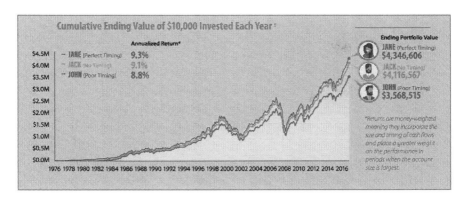

Fact No.4: Missing out on the best days is even worse

Trying to time the market is extremely difficult to do. There is almost no trader that can perfectly time their buys at the low and sells at the highs. **Missing out on the best days** just because you are **trying to time the market** either by trying to buy at the lows, or even worse still, trading (buy at the lows and sell at the highs consecutively) **is even worse**. The analysis from J. P. Morgan Asset Management[4] clearly shows that **just missing out on the 10 and 20 best days** cuts your portfolio returns from a 20-year investing period **from 6.06%** to an absolutely **horrendous 2.44% and 0.08% respectively**.

Unfortunately, **most of us are likely not perfect timers** (maybe 99.9%? of us, ask any top traders you know, and you can confirm what I am saying). Why time the market when **it will inherently lower your probability of success** and worsen your outcomes? Thus, **don't try to time the market for your long-term investments**. Market lows often result in emotional decision making. Investing for the long term while managing volatility can and will more likely result in a better investment outcome.

---

[4] Source: J.P. Morgan Asset Management, Guide to Retirement 2020 - (slide 43) https://am.jpmorgan.com/blob-gim/1383421113847/83456/JPM%20-%20 2020%20Guide%20to%20Retirement.pdf

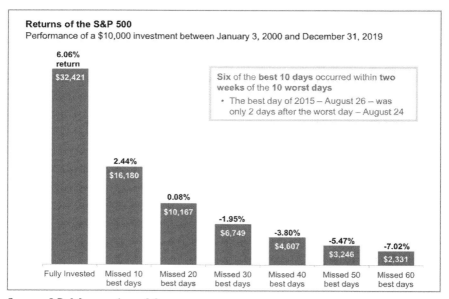

Returns of the S&P 500
Performance of a $10,000 investment between January 3, 2000 and December 31, 2019

Six of the **best 10 days** occurred within **two weeks** of the 10 **worst days**
• The best day of 2015 — August 26 — was only 2 days after the worst day — August 24

Source: J.P. Morgan Asset Management

Years of experience have taught me that there is **no Holy Grail of market timing** where **one consistently buys at the bottom and sells at the top**. Or at least if there is one, I haven't found it.

Commitment No. 1

We will not market time or trade with respect to our long-term investments.

QUICK SUMMARY

- Be an **investor rather than a trader**. Investors profit using a **buy and hold** and looking only at the long term, which is the only term that counts...
- Accept that no one can accurately **predict the market**, including you.
- Attempts to **time the market** to buy at the lows and sell at the highs leads to loss.
- It is **better to be fully invested** than to miss out on the best days.

CHAPTER 3

WHY NOT ACTIVE-MANAGED MUTUAL FUNDS OR UNIT TRUSTS?

Fact No.1: Most professionals cannot even beat the diversified S&P 500 Index

> *"A blindfolded monkey throwing darts*
> *at a newspaper's financial pages*
> *could select a portfolio that would do just as well*
> *as one carefully selected by experts."*

- Burton G. Malkiel, *A Random Walk Down Wall Street:*
The Time-Tested Strategy for Successful Investing

Warren Buffett once bet a million U.S. dollars that **no investment professional** would be able to choose a basket of high-fee, complex hedge funds that could **outperform a simple, broadly diversified equity index fund over a ten-year period**.

Only one person stepped up to the challenge: Ted Seides of Protégé Partners. To cut a long story short, **Seides conceded defeat in May 2017, six months before the ten-year deadline.** At that point, Buffett's chosen index fund, the Vanguard S&P 500, was up over 80% in returns, while

Seides' basket of selected hedge funds was only up around 20%. Buffett has long been an opponent of hedge funds and other high-fee investment businesses, saying that they provide no value to investors. At the 2016 Berkshire shareholders' meeting, he said: "There's been far, far more money made by people in Wall Street through salesmanship abilities than through investment abilities."

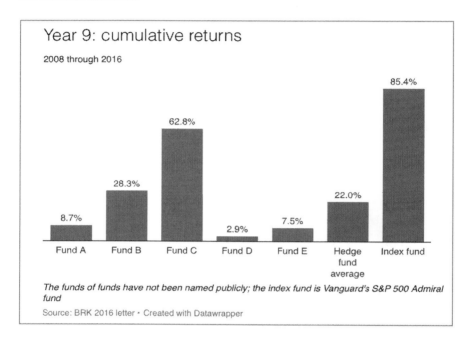

Year 9: cumulative returns

2008 through 2016

The funds of funds have not been named publicly; the index fund is Vanguard's S&P 500 Admiral fund

Source: BRK 2016 letter · Created with Datawrapper

Let's not forget that Buffett himself is a great active manager. He has beaten stock market indices for many years in a row and has a good eye for value when he sees it. He says that **it is possible to beat the index**, but he **knows only a handful of top investment professionals who can do so**. The ordinary investor simply does not possess the guile or behavioral capacity to do the same. But is that true? Let's look at the evidence.

Before we start, it is important to clarify the **difference between unit trusts and mutual funds**. Fundamentally they both are similar—the fund managers invest funds in various assets (equities and fixed income) to meet a particular financial objective (i.e. to outperform a particular benchmark).

A **unit trust fund** is an investment scheme that pools money from investors to meet a specific financial objective. The manager of the fund then invests the money in various securities such as shares or bonds, with the hope of meeting the desired objective of the fund.

Mutual funds are investment schemes, very similar to unit trusts, found in the United States and a few other countries. Though there are three different types of mutual funds i.e. open-ended, unit investment trust, and closed-ended, the most common is the open-ended fund. They work on the same principle as a unit trust. So, we can say that it is similar but not quite the same.

The **main difference** between the two is in their **legal structure**. A **mutual fund** is an investment company that **issues redeemable shares** while a **unit trust,** because it is not a company, only **issues units**.

Examples of mutual fund companies are Fidelity Investments – where the famous Peter Lynch once ran the Fidelity's Magellan Fund – and Vanguard Group (both based in the USA).

Interestingly, there are over 15,000 mutual funds in the US compared to only 2,800 listed securities on the New York Stock Exchange! This suggests that **two of the surest ways to make money from mutual funds are to run and sell them**!

Fact No. 2: Majority of active funds (53-94%) fail to beat the market

The following chart from SPIVA research[5] clearly illustrates this. Most of the active funds in the world ranging **from 53% to 94% underperform their benchmarks**.

---

[5] Source: SPIVA,
S&P Dow Jones Indices LLC, Morningstar, Fundata, CRSP. Data as of June 30, 2019.
https://us.spindices.com/documents/spiva/spiva-infographic.pdf?force_download=true

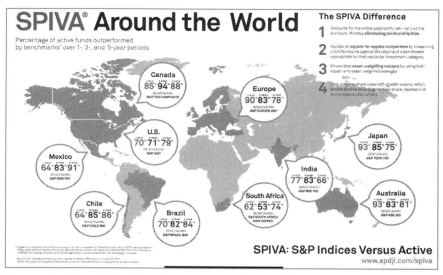

Source: SPIVA (S&P Indices Versus Active), data as of June 30, 2019

Fact No.3: Most winning funds are unable to continue winning

In fact, another SPIVA Research[6] shows that irrespective of asset class or style focus, **few fund managers consistently outperformed their peers**. In fact, an inverse relationship exists between the time horizon length and the ability of top-performing funds to maintain their success. In simple

---

[6] **SPIVA Research - Does Past Performance Matter? The Persistence Scorecard (December 2019)** https://us.spindices.com/documents/spiva/persistence-score-card-december-2019.pdf?force_download=true

Since 2001, S&P Dow Jones Indices has released its annual SPIVA U.S. Scorecard report, which examines the performance of fund managers relative to their most closely linked benchmark index.

Whereas most funds are often compared to the performance of the broad-based S&P 500, this does not always equate to an accurate comparison, especially if it's a small-cap growth fund or say a real estate fund. The SPIVA U.S. Scorecard adjusts for this, and other factors, to give investors an encompassing look at how the professional fund managers are really performing over one-, three-, five-, 10-, and 15-year time frames, relative to their benchmark.

words, **most (97%) top-performing active funds do not continue to be top-performing after 5 years**.

1. **Less than 3% of equity funds in all categories** maintained their **top-quartile** status at the end of the five-year measurement period.
2. **Less than 13% of equity funds in all categories** maintained their **top-half** status at the end of the five-year measurement period.
3. In fact, **no large-cap fund was able to consistently deliver top-quartile performance by the end of the fifth year.**

Report 2: Performance Persistence of Domestic Equity Funds over Five Consecutive 12-Month Periods

MUTUAL FUND CATEGORY	FUND COUNT AT START (SEPTEMBER 2015)	PERCENTAGE REMAINING IN TOP QUARTILE			
		SEPTEMBER 2016	SEPTEMBER 2017	SEPTEMBER 2018	SEPTEMBER 2019
TOP QUARTILE					
All Domestic Funds	567	17.64	6.53	4.06	0.88
All Large-Cap Funds	220	14.09	6.36	5.00	0.00
All Mid-Cap Funds	80	16.25	1.25	1.25	1.25
All Small-Cap Funds	132	20.45	7.58	3.79	1.52
All Multi-Cap Funds	135	17.04	10.37	6.67	2.22
MUTUAL FUND CATEGORY	FUND COUNT AT START (SEPTEMBER 2015)	PERCENTAGE REMAINING IN TOP HALF			
		SEPTEMBER 2016	SEPTEMBER 2017	SEPTEMBER 2018	SEPTEMBER 2019
TOP HALF					
All Domestic Funds	1135	45.64	24.49	16.83	8.37
All Large-Cap Funds	440	41.82	20.00	15.68	6.36
All Mid-Cap Funds	160	40.62	18.75	15.00	12.50
All Small-Cap Funds	265	44.15	23.02	13.96	7.55
All Multi-Cap Funds	270	43.70	21.85	16.67	8.89

Source: S&P Dow Jones Indices LLC, CRSP. Data as of Sept. 30, 2019. Table is provided for illustrative purposes. Past performance is no guarantee of future results.

Fact No.4: When we look at longer time frames, the effect is amplified

Professionals **struggle even harder to beat the market as time goes by**. 639*-

In a study by Dimensional Fund Advisors LP on US-Based Mutual Funds, they concluded that:

1. **Outperforming funds** were in the **minority**.
2. **Strong track records failed to persist.**

3. **High costs** and **excessive turnover** may have contributed to **underperformance**.

> *"**Wall Street** is the only place that **people ride to in a Rolls Royce to get advice from those who take the subway**."*
> *- Warren Buffett*

*When trillions of dollars are managed by Wall Streeters charging high fees, it will usually be the **managers who reap outsized profits, not the clients**."*
- Warren Buffett

> *"If returns are going to be 7 or 8 percent and you're **paying 1 percent for fees**, that makes an **enormous difference** in how much money you're going to have in retirement."*
> *- Warren Buffett*

Specifically, they found that:

1. Only about **half of the pros (51%) survive** and worse, **only 1 in 5 beat the market after 15 years.**
2. **51% of equity** mutual funds and **55% of fixed income** funds **survived but unperformed** their benchmarks **over the past 15 years.**
3. **Only 14% of equity** mutual funds **and 13% of fixed income** funds **both survived and outperformed** their benchmarks **over the past 15 years.**

To find a **US-based mutual fund** that is **still around and has outperformed its benchmark over the past 15 years** is approximately **1 in 7.**

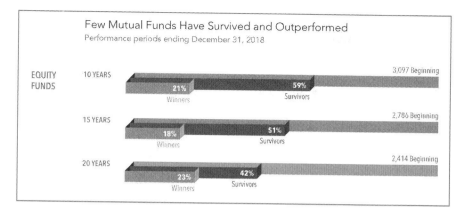

Few Mutual Funds Have Survived and Outperformed
Performance periods ending December 31, 2018

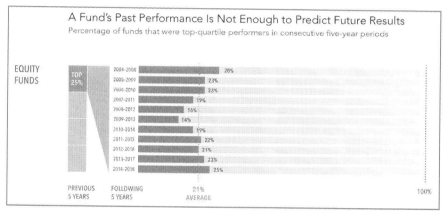

A Fund's Past Performance Is Not Enough to Predict Future Results
Percentage of funds that were top-quartile performers in consecutive five-year periods

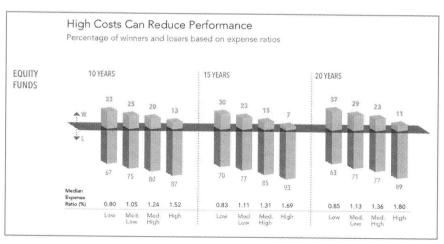

High Costs Can Reduce Performance
Percentage of winners and losers based on expense ratios

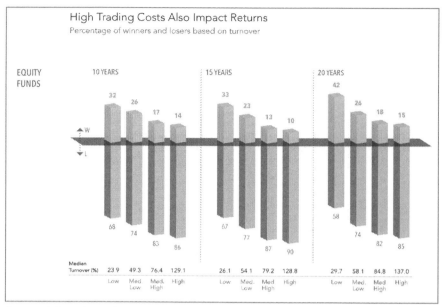

Source: Mutual Fund Landscape 2019[7] by Dimensional Fund Advisors LP.

Fact No.5: Most finance professionals struggle to beat the S&P 500 and it only gets worse over time

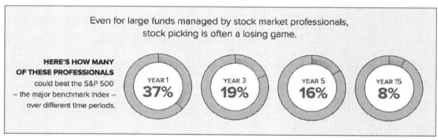

Source: J.P. Morgan

In addition, **another reason to avoid mutual funds** is that in most cases, you **cannot see the business in which you are investing**. If we apply the principle **"Don't invest in something that I do not fully understand,"** then we should cross 90% of all mutual funds off our shortlist. Thus, when

---

[7] **Mutual Fund Landscape 2019** by Dimensional Fund Advisors LP
https://hub.dimensional.com/exLink.asp?40838454OC19S68I88753842

you cannot see what is going on with your money, it doesn't matter because you cannot evaluate a fund's holdings or strategy, you can only pay your money and take your chances. But more importantly, **why take a chance and invest in mutual funds when the odds are so stacked against you?**

Reason 1: Size of capital working against fund managers

Ask any number of fund managers whether they **can get better returns with a $50,000 portfolio** or a $5 billion portfolio, and most if not, all **will say the former**. It is no easy road for fund managers. But what is it so tough for them? The chief reason is they find it **difficult to invest at scale** in one of the most rewarding segments: **smaller companies**. A fund of $10bn in assets under management (AUM) cannot invest $500mil (5% of their capital) in a company whose market capitalization is only $1bn.

The smaller investor can, however, make money by investing in these smaller companies without driving up the share price significantly. But not the much larger fund managers when they are managing portfolios in the hundreds of millions if not billions of dollars. It is **far easier for a small-cap company to grow 10X** from $1bn to $10bn in market capitalization and experiencing revenue and earnings growth in excess of 50% p.a. It is definitely much more challenging (though not impossible) for a **large-cap company to double their existing $500bn Market Capitalization** to $1 trillion because as these companies scale and become larger, they tend to **experience slowing rates of growth**.

Reason 2: Their source of capital is not long-term enough

When **markets go up**, investors want to **give you more capital to invest for them**. But that is when valuations tend to be more expensive. Vice versa, when **markets go down**, investors want to **withdraw and end up taking away capital from you**, forcing you to sell your holdings to liquidate to return their capital, when they should be going in to scoop up companies at low valuations. Structurally, **fund managers are forced to buy high and sell low**, and never able to add and buy more when there are market sell-offs. Some of the fund managers do have lock-in periods, but this is not typically common in the mutual fund business. This structural disadvantage makes it so much harder for equity fund managers to outperform and beat the market.

Markets take capital away from fund managers when they don't need it (at the lows) **and give it to them when they shouldn't be adding to it** (at the highs)**.** The following chart highlights the positive correlation between the stock market vs equity fund inflows and outflows.

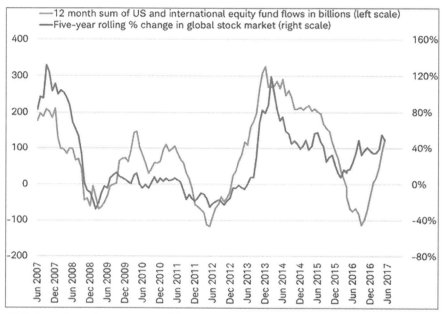

Global stock market represented by MSCI AC World Index[8]

In short, the average professional investor fails to beat the market and finds it difficult to identify a consistent few that keeps beating the market.

We hope that this collection of data we presented earlier **has made you reconsider investing or continue to invest in mutual funds, active**

---

[8] Source: Source: Charles Schwab, Bloomberg and Investment Company Institute data as of 8/5/2017 https://finance.yahoo.com/news/what-are-fund-flows-telling-us-about-trends-and-201936072.html

funds, or managed funds and the like. More importantly, we hope you are now more educated, and you want to learn the ropes of investing for yourself. Because I am sure you can. If I can, surely you can.

QUICK SUMMARY

- Choose **index funds** over mutual funds, active funds, or managed funds.
- With mutual funds, you can't see the business **you're investing in**.
- Up to 94% of active funds **fail to beat the market**.
- 97% of top performing **active funds decline in five years**.
- Most **finance professionals** can't beat the S&P 500.
- Take advantage of your smaller investor status by **investing in smaller companies.**

CHAPTER 4

WHY NOT PASSIVELY-MANAGED INDEX FUNDS AND ETFS?

What Is an S&P 500 Index Fund?

The **S&P 500** is a market-cap weighted index of 500 of the **largest and most profitable companies in the U.S.**

An S&P 500 index fund is an investment vehicle, either in a mutual fund or exchange-traded fund (ETF) form, that invests in the 500 stocks that comprise the S&P 500 equity index, in market-cap-weighted proportions.

While fees vary, these tend to be extremely cheap ways to invest. As of this writing, the S&P 500 ETFs can be found with expense ratios as low as 0.03%. This means that for every $10,000 you have invested, fees will only be $3 per year.

Warren Buffett's Favorite Investment: S&P 500 ETF

Billionaire and legendary investor **Warren Buffett** said that an **S&P 500 index fund is the best investment most Americans can make**. In fact, he's said that he wants his own wife's money invested in such a fund after he's gone. This might seem a bit surprising, as Buffett is well-known for his stock-picking ability.

First of all, Warren Buffett **isn't necessarily saying that it's a bad idea to buy individual stocks**. But **if and only if you have the time, knowledge, and desire to do it right**. However, **most Americans don't**.

Essentially, Buffett feels that an investment in an S&P 500 index fund is a bet on American business, which has historically been a very good one. Over the long run, the S&P 500 has generated total returns of about 10% annualized.

And since S&P 500 index funds generally have minimal fees, you get to keep the vast majority of the returns. In a nutshell, an S&P 500 index fund guarantees that you'll do as well as the market over time, which has historically been quite good.

Good Years and Bad

To be clear, Warren Buffett is a **fan of S&P 500 index funds as a long-term investment**. In other words, if you will need the money you are investing within a few years, you're better off looking elsewhere, such as shorter tenor, bank deposits, five-year certificate of deposits (CD), or bonds.

The reason for this is that the S&P 500, just like individual stocks, can be quite volatile over shorter periods of time. Over the past 50 years, the index has gained 30% or more in nine separate years but has also lost as much as 37% in a single year, even after factoring in dividends. However, over long periods of time—say, 20 years or more—the S&P 500 has never been a bad choice.

How Much Would $10,000 in 1980 Be Worth Today?

To illustrate this, let's say that you had invested $10,000 in a low-cost S&P 500 index fund in 1980. Since January 1, 1980, the S&P 500 index has generated a total return of approximately 7,670% as of February 1, 2018. This translates to a 12.1% annualized rate of return.

Assuming an expense ratio of 0.1% on your index fund (you can find even lower costs now), this means that a **$10,000 investment** would have **turned into just over $760,000 as of February 1, 2018**.

This is why Warren Buffett loves cheap index funds as an investment for the majority of investors. Sure, **you would not have beaten the market**, **but you would have been guaranteed to do just as well as the market**. An S&P 500 index fund would have allowed any investor to turn $10,000 into more than three-quarters of a million dollars in less than four decades—with the **bare minimum of effort and expense**.

Shift Away from Managed Active Investing to Passive Investing

Vanguard Group founder Jack Bogle, who died on Jan 16, 2019 at age 89, ushered in an era of low-cost investing for the many. Jack Bogle launched the first index mutual fund for individual investors at the end of 1975 for the purpose of passive investing; **skip the stock-picking**, **save on fees**, and **simply ride the ups and downs** of the overall market. His fringe idea became mainstream.

Assets in **passively managed** U.S. equity funds are likely or could have already **surpassed assets in actively managed** ones. By pushing down fees across the industry, Bogle may have saved American investors $1 trillion over his lifetime, calculates Bloomberg intelligence analyst Eric Balchunas. Bogle **theorized you can't reliably beat the market**, you **might as well join it, be the market, and settle for average performance**.

This has some truth to it, as we saw earlier, depending on time horizons, only a small percentage, **18-23% of active managed funds have beaten the benchmarks** over the last 10, 15, and 20 years.

And true enough, because **since most fund managers cannot even beat the market**, the **investor should just buy an index fund/ETF** and **accept that market average returns are the best that one can do**. Vanguard (with CEO Jack Bogle) has been one of the great successes for investors over the past 30 years, **attracting literally trillions of dollars of investments to the index fund and the ETF cause**.

Money has effectively become "dumber and dumber" over time as the chart from BloombergQuint clearly makes the point. New capital from investors just goes into passively managed ETFs, which just then goes into buying all the respective stock constituents.

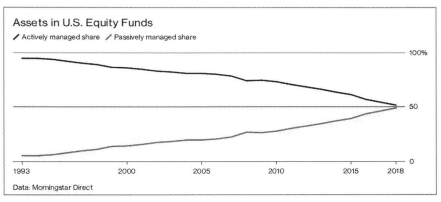

Source: BloombergQuint[9]

Do You Want to Be Just Average?

There's an extraordinarily important and rudimentary lesson that the vast majority of private investors still have yet to learn: "**If you can't beat 'em, join 'em.**" And that is why there is a lot of sense to just buy or invest in passively managed low-cost ETFs with a regular investment at frequent intervals (without market timing) framework. Vanguard, iShares, and State Street are the three largest (see below) and they are there to help you. Fees have also decreased over time and that is definitely a plus.

---

[9] Source: Bloomberg. https://www.bloombergquint.com/businessweek/index-funds-are-king-but-some-indexers-are-passive-aggressive

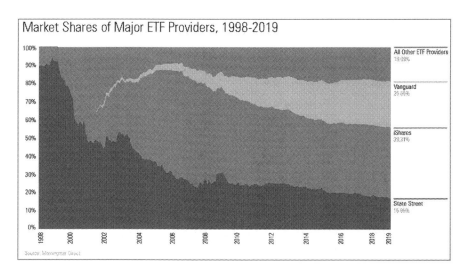

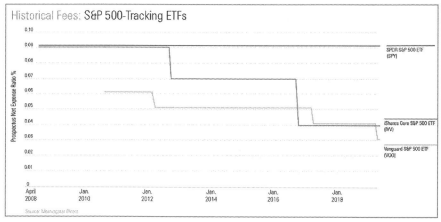

Source: Morningstar[10]

But by definition, because there are **still fees in ETFs, though how low it may be** (e.g. Vanguard is at 0.03%), **ETFs will still never beat the stock market**. The following two 3-year and 5-year graphs from YCharts clearly bring across the case in point.

---

[10] Source: Morningstar (ETF Market Share: The Competitive Landscape of the Top Three Firms)
https://www.morningstar.com/insights/2019/08/01/etf-market-share

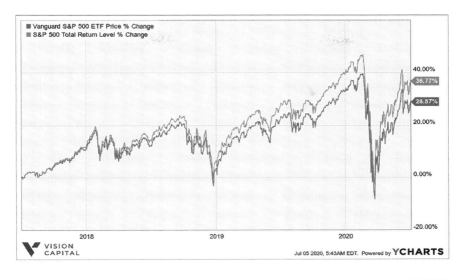

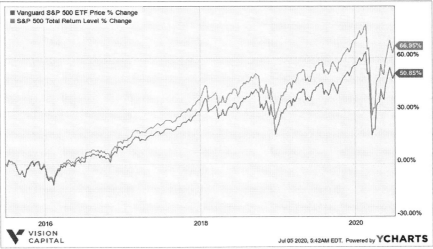

Source: YCharts as of July 05, 2020

If you think that's all that you want to do with respect to your investments which will likely count for approximately ~20-30% of your net worth as your wealth grows, and that beating ~75-80% of Wall Street professionals is good enough for you, you can stop here and discontinue reading. But really…you did not buy this book just to be average right?

Managing money and mastering how we manage our money is key to our wealth and financial success. We firmly believe **you can do better than just average** (though it is not easy to be average) by investing in ETFs and index funds.

Do you prefer to tell your grandchildren a story that you had been one of the greatest investors who ever lived, building your wealth and bene-fiting massively financially by **investing and owning some of the best companies that ever existed** or investing in ETFs? We prefer to invest our money to be **smarter, richer, and happier,** and we think you can and want to do so as well.

In the following chapters, we hope to **change your beliefs and mindsets** concerning long-term Investing and provide a comprehensive approach for you to start, such that the **probability of winning** and **better outcomes** is **more likely to be in your favor** rather than stacked against you.

Commitment No. 2

We commit and know we can invest better and beat the market.

Why Individual Equities You Might Ask?

Because today, you are armed with **more information, greater and cheaper access** to the markets than ever before. Today, you can find a stock idea, research it online, and buy the shares, **all in a matter of min-utes if not seconds**...not that we think you should.

But much remains the same. **Investing in individual equities remains one of the truest paths to lasting wealth**. Many Wall Street and finance professionals will argue to their last breath that you cannot and are unable to do it on your own (and that's why you need them!) But there is **clear evidence** that **individual investors can beat the market**...so long as you can overcome a few key behavioral barriers. A change in your belief system (BS) and mindset will be needed, but let's get there later shall we?

Deeply inspired by The Motley Fool, we want to **go where other investors would not**, to **do what other investors do not**. We want to **educate, to amuse, and to enrich**. We want to **Help The World Invest Better**, so **we can be Smarter, Happier, and Richer**. We are shepherds of our capital, and with it, we want to drive our capital to support businesses that create long-term positive sustainable value and in turn, **make the world and mankind better than when we first started**.

My goal is very simple: **to beat the market and show others how to do it**. Whether you are a teenager or a student in school wanting to invest the proceeds from your part-time or summer job for the first time, or if you are just starting your working career and have not invested before, or you've tried but have not been successful at it, or if you've been working for a number of years already, we hope this book will help you start your path and set a course towards the financial future you seek.

Our approach will be best characterized by our **general disinterest in and mild disdain for conventional wisdom**. For example, finance professionals will encourage you to invest your money in loaded mutual funds/unit trusts. This enables them to charge you twice from that advice and then on an annual basis for the fund management fees. The recent rhetoric in the finance world with Jack Bogle, Warren Buffett, and many others have shifted this towards index funds and more so towards low-cost exchange-traded funds (ETFs). There is some truth in this, the argument goes along like this: **if you cannot beat the market** (average) and most cannot anyway, why not join them and **invest via ETFs** and get the **market (average)** return?

Now surely, we did not get you to purchase this book just to invest in ETFs and just be average right? Because we believe **you are not just average**, you can be better than that. In fact, **you can be above average and beat the market (over the long run)** where the majority of financial professionals have failed. But that definitely will not be via any managed or mutual funds/unit trusts where someone manages your money.

We, on the other hand, are **telling you to buy stocks**. Now, some finance professionals from your stock brokerage or sell-side investment banks might tell you to **buy the stock of the month** (e.g. move to utilities as the market is heading into a downturn, move to oil companies with rising oil prices, rotate to cyclicals and consumer plays with the economic recovery, turnarounds, etc.). Sounds familiar? Or you might have others recommend that you only buy the safest stocks and preferably undervalued with a margin of safety towards the world of value investing. But this book is not about that. In fact, if you disagree, you should stop and not continue reading.

Buy Great, Not Mediocre

But instead, this book is about you **buying shares of great companies** with a solid array of core strong companies while sprinkling some of your capital on more volatile growth stocks. Skip the penny stocks, turnarounds, the flavor of the month, and any business that you cannot explain in under 1 minute (outside of your circle of competence). Then **hold these stocks for the long haul—think decades and years**, not months, weeks, days, and definitely not hours or minutes. We want you to be a **shareholder, investing and owning in some of the best possible businesses out there**, not buying a stock ticker.

We advocate this approach for **one simple reason: it works**. Going back through history, you will see that the stock market is **pretty close to a sure thing**, if you **have the proper time** (no day trading and keep buying and selling) **and temperament** (no panicking during selloffs, selling off everything, and being overly optimistic and buying more when markets are at a record high trying to chase the market).

These are the questions we would like to start thinking about as we read through the next section:

1. If the pros can't consistently beat the market, can we still beat the market?
2. And if we can? How do we go about doing it?

3. What are the facts telling us? What are the key factors we should be looking at?

4. Can we put together a framework and principles to identify these winners and invest in them?

QUICK SUMMARY

- An S&P 500 index fund is an **investment vehicle** that ensures you'll do **as well as the market** in the long run.
- Make the switch from managed active investing to **passive investing.**
- Be better than average by **investing in ETFs and index funds**.
- Investing in **individual equities** is the clearest path to wealth.
- Buy shares in **great companies** and hold them.

C H A P T E R 5

WHY INVESTING IS A GAME OF MATHEMATICS

Understanding and winning at the game of investing requires one to **understand the mathematics behind probabilities and outcomes.**

This entire book and the following chapters are meant to drive you to an approach to relook at investing and to **swing the odds in your favor**, such that as you start investing or looking to invest more, you are going in with a **much higher chance of winning** and **winning with even bigger gains.** Ultimately, we want you **to outperform and beat the market over the long run** (because that's the only horizon that counts). We are confident that you can do so if you apply the timeless principles set out in this book and stick to them religiously.

Why Long Term Is the Only Term That Counts?

Look at the **four long-term charts of the S&P 500**[11] provided in the following pages, the **stock market in general over the long run** has **always**

---

[11] **What is the S&P 500 index?** The S&P 500 index is a basket of 500 of the largest U.S. stocks, weighted by market capitalization. The index is widely considered to be the best indicator of how large U.S. stocks are performing on a day-to-day basis.

risen with time and **starts in the lower left, it goes to the upper right of each chart.**

*"In the **short-term**, the market **can go down faster than it goes up**.*
*But over the **long-term**, the market **goes up more than it goes down**.*
*The **long run is the only term that counts and matters to us**."*
- Eugene Ng (adapted from David Gardner)

S&P 500: From Inception (since 1950)

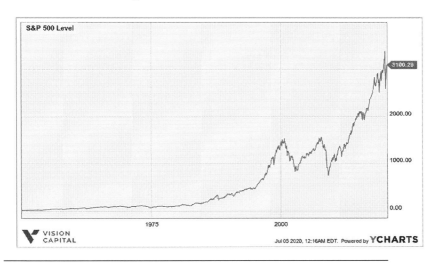

The 500 large-cap U.S. stocks account for about 80% of all U.S. publicly traded market capitalization.

To be added to the S&P 500, the following criteria must be met:
1) It must be a **U.S. company**.
2) The **market cap** must be **$5.3 billion or more**.
3) The **public float** must consist of **at least 50%** of outstanding shares.
4) It **must have positive reported earnings in the most recent quarter**, as well as over the four most recent quarters.
5) The stock must have an **active market** and must **trade for a reasonable share price**.

Meeting these criteria isn't a guarantee that a stock will join the S&P 500 -- these are just the minimum requirements.

Source: https://www.fool.com/knowledge-center/what-is-the-sp-500.aspx

S&P 500: 40-Year Chart

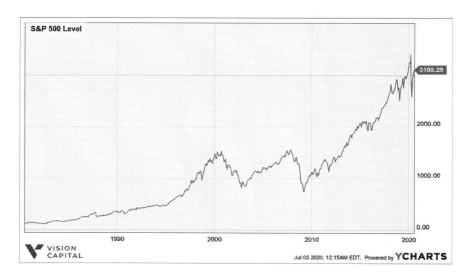

S&P 500: 20-Year Chart

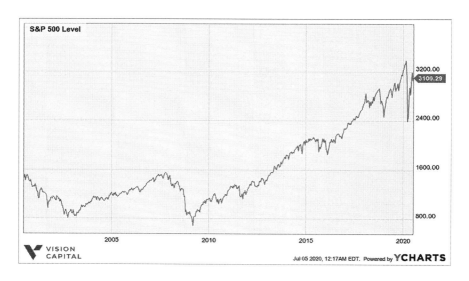

S&P 500: 10-Year Chart

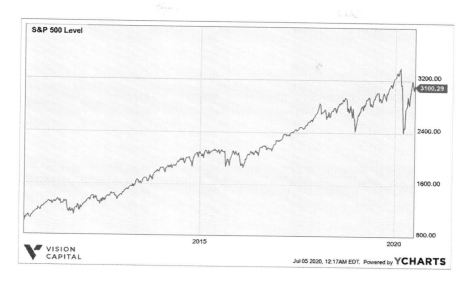

Why Stocks Always Go up More Than They Go Down?

It becomes self-evident from the graphs of the stock market over the last century. It starts in the lower left; it goes to the upper right. That is the reality. And that is highly likely what will happen in the next century. **We will continue creating value for each other. That's what we do through business.** And then **we can co-own each other's enterprises. That's what we do in the stock market.** And as we continue to innovate, we continue to improve the world and find better ways to serve you and me more cheaply or more amazingly. That's the story of capitalism done well. And it ends up resulting in decades and a century of gains. **That's why stocks always go up more than they go down.**

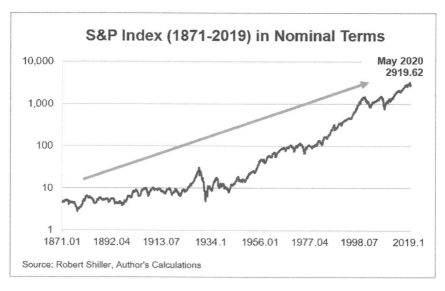

Source: Robert Shiller[12], Author's calculations

---

[12] Source: http://www.econ.yale.edu/~shiller/data.htm

There Are Always Geopolitical Conflicts and Disasters

The finance world often argues that the world is currently facing danger-ous geopolitical upheavals and disaster waiting to happen, or that it is too late to catch up with an expansion that has already gone on for ten years. Conflicts may bring the world to the edge of the abyss again and again, but they never mean the end. Every time, people and companies once again manage to defy such situations and make it through. That is the **beauty of mankind. We are resilient and always get back on our feet—as do the stock markets**.

Why the Long-Term Is Really the Only Term That Counts?

The **following chart is probably the most important in the entire book**, and I would like you to spend some time, look at it, and understand what it means for you.

Invest for the long-term where Wall Street does not play. Timing the market is a fool's game; it is **time in the market that is truly your greatest advantage** that you have over Wall Street and many finance pro-fessionals. It is **time in the market** that is **the biggest secret to investing successfully**.

Source: Robert Shiller[13], Bloomberg, Author's calculations

> "**Timing the market is a fool's game.**
> Whereas **time in the market is your greatest advantage.**
> - Nick Murray"

> *"When we own portions of **outstanding businesses**
> **with outstanding managements,**
> **our favorite holding period is forever."**
> - Warren Buffett*

It's pretty clear, right? The **odds of success** in any period **less than about five years** are **between a coin toss and an OK bet** (~61-79%). It's **not until you're investing for 10 years or more that the odds of success are overwhelmingly in your favor** (~81-100%, yes 100%!). One of my strong beliefs as an investor is that when progress is measured generationally, performance should not be measured hourly, daily, weekly, monthly, or even quarterly. Good investing means looking for situations where the odds of success are in your favor. Few things increase those odds more than extending your patience.

---

[13] Source: http://www.econ.yale.edu/~shiller/data.htm

The longer your investment holding horizon, the higher the probability you will have a positive return. In fact, holding periods of a single day were essentially a coin toss (52% of those days earned positive returns with a slight positive skew). But investors with longer horizons fared much, much better. 88% of 10-year holding periods were positive (not a typo) and 100% of 20 and 30-year holding periods made money.

So, **do not invest in the short-term** (up to 1-2 years) where Wall Street plays, better still, don't try trading and timing your buy and sells. **Investing long-term is the advantage you have** that Wall Street does not, so make full use of that advantage. **Tilt the mathematics, probability, and odds of making money investing in your favor. Investing with horizons greater than 10 years (or even longer) is the first secret.**

Do you want to **play a game with a loaded dice that 88-100% of the time you will win?** I definitely would want that for sure. Do you? As George Soros rightly says: "If investing is entertaining, if you're having fun, you're probably not making any money. Good investing is boring." If you want excitement, go to the casino (not that I am advocating…), go skydiving, take a rollercoaster ride, do whatever you want. But just don't do it when it comes to your investments. Just leave it alone.

The below chart by J.P. Morgan Asset Management is especially instructive. If you invest with 10 year and 20-year horizons, a 100% stock portfolio returns +19% to -1% p.a. for 10 year rolling periods and +17% to +6% p.a. for 20-year rolling periods. This means that if you had **invested for 20-year horizons and beyond, you would have never lost any money** and the **only question is how much money you would have made instead.** Now, isn't that a better problem to have?

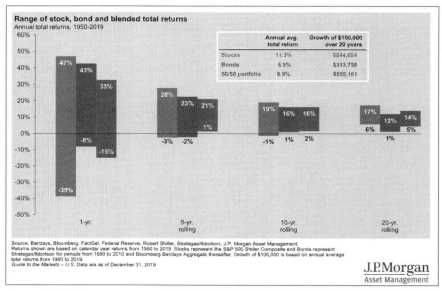

Source: J.P. Morgan Asset Management, Guide to the Markets[14]

Once you **get your fundamentals right**, the **second secret** is that all you need is to find the **best possible companies that are likely to win over the long-term and invest in them**. Now isn't that a better way to invest?

Thus, if you have the **patience and fortitude** to **hold on to your investments for 10 or 20 years and longer,** your prospects become much brighter. You'll ride out the short-term noise and **benefit from the long-term upwards trend**.

As always, Warren Buffet put it best: "**The stock market is a device for transferring money from the impatient to the patient.**"

Commitment No. 3

When we invest, we invest only for the long-term. Our holding period is forever.

---

[14] Source: J.P. Morgan Asset Management, Guide to the Markets
https://am.jpmorgan.com/blobcontent/1383654213584/83456/MI-GT-M_1Q20.pdf

Investing in Equities Return on Average 7-9% over the Very Long Run

With the U.S. representing ~25% of global GDP and U.S. companies making up ~50% of global equity indices, the long-term performance of our investments will be heavily influenced by the overall state of the U.S. market. The annual returns of the U.S. stock market across the full 147 years are shown below. Overall, the simple average return across the time period has been **8.4%** per year, while the annualized return (also known as the geometric return) from start to finish has been **6.8%** per year.

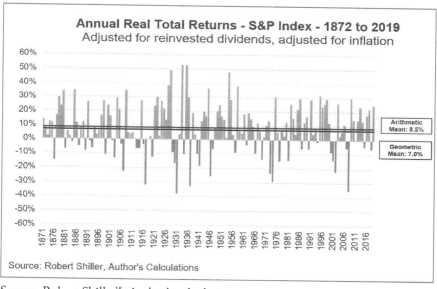

Source: Robert Shiller, Author's Calculations

Source: Robert Shiller[15], Author's calculations

The Stock Market Is Volatile, but It Is More Likely to Go Up Than Down

> *"Stocks will always go down faster than they go up,*
> *but stocks will go up more than they go down over time."*
> *- David Gardner, The Motley Fool*

---

[15] Source: http://www.econ.yale.edu/~shiller/data.htm

Looking at the distribution of annual returns of the S&P 500, while the U.S. stock market has trended upwards over time, ~31% of years on record have had negative returns. Thus, on average, we can expect **7 in 10 years to be a positive year** and **3 in 10 years to be a negative year**.

> *"Unless you can watch your stock holdings*
> *decline by 50% without becoming panic-stricken,*
> *you should not be in the stock market."*
> *— Warren Buffett*

The **returns in any single year can be extremely volatile**. The market has lost between 30-40% in five different years (1917, 1931, 1937, 1974, 2008), while the market has gained more than 50% twice (1933 and 1954).

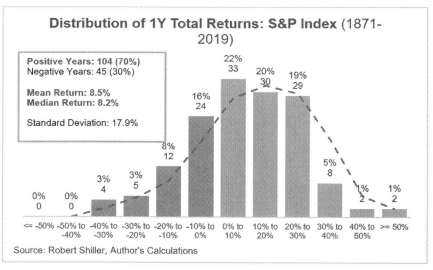

Source: Robert Shiller[16], Author's calculations

How Often and by How Much Does the Stock Market Go Down?

This is our second favorite chart in the entire book because this plays an extremely important part of how we feel and react towards investing.

---

[16] Source: http://www.econ.yale.edu/~shiller/data.htm

We know that the **market will fall from time to time** (we know it will, but **don't know when exactly**), but we know **by how much and how often**. We need to **come to expect that this will happen all the time**, and <u>**market drops are just part and parcel of investing**</u>. Thus, we frame our minds to expect volatility and use market drops as opportunities to add to our high conviction companies.

Market falls by this much	Historical frequency
10%	Every 1 year
15%	Every 2 years
20%	Every 4 years
30%	Every 10 years
40%	Every 10-30 years
50%	2-3 times every 100 years

Source: Author's calculations, S&P 500 data since 1928

Market declines are very common, and must be expected. In fact, **~93% of the time, the market** (i.e. S&P 500) **is below its historical high**. When you start investing, it will often feel like you are experiencing a loss.

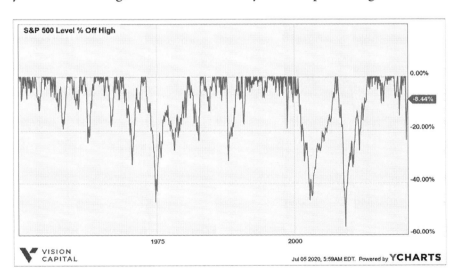

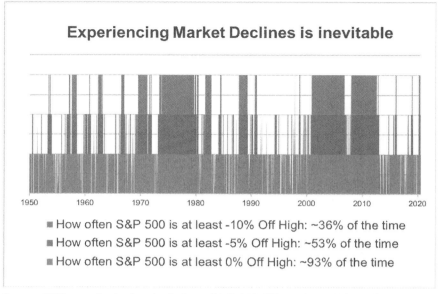

Source: YCharts, Author's calculations, S&P 500 (4Jan1950 – 1Jul2020)

Market declines are part and parcel for any rising stock market.

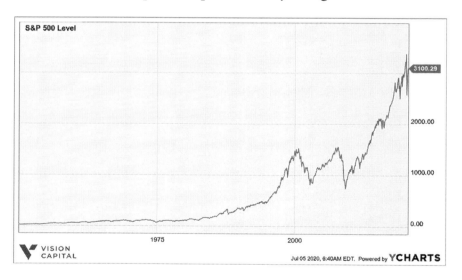

The only thing we are **100% absolutely sure** about the market is that "**It will fluctuate.**"

1. We understand that **stocks produce superior long-term returns** at the **cost of higher volatility.**
2. Whenever there is volatility and massive market sell-offs, ask yourself: **"What is going on? Has anything changed? Is this a temporary setback or something more permanent?"**
3. **"Nine out of ten times**, the answer will probably be the same: **Nothing is going on. This is just what stocks do."**

Why Is It Better to Have More Expectations and Fewer Forecasts?

It is **better to have no idea what happens next** than to believe you know exactly what will happen, thus setting yourself up for disappointment and dangerous behaviors.

If I say, "The next recession will begin in 2024," I've made a forecast.

If I say, "Recessions occur roughly every 5-10 years," I've expressed an expectation.

They seem similar, but they're very different.

Forecasts rely on knowing when something will occur. **Expectations are an acknowledgment of what's likely to occur without professing insight into when it will happen.**

Expectations are healthier than forecasts because they provide a vision of the future stripped of all false precision. If you know a recession will occur at some point, you won't be that surprised whenever it arrives—which is a huge benefit. But if you assume you know exactly when it will occur, you'll be tempted into all kinds of dangerous behavior, leveraged with overconfidence. And you'll be shocked when time passes and what you thought would occur didn't (yet).

Here's a useful expectation: **assume the market will fall massively (20-50%) once or twice every 5-10 years and smaller falls (10-20%) once**

every 1-5 years. <u>I don't know where, when, how, or who will cause it to happen</u>. But when you expect the world to break every once in a while, you prepare for events you can't foresee, and **you don't have to rewrite your playbook when they happen**. You'll prefer big cushions and room for error. When people ask, "What are you preparing for?" you'll say, "A world that history shows are both a growth machine and a continuous chain of unforeseen agony." A world **where we have no idea what will happen next**. Nothing more specific.

That is why the best investors in the world (Warren Buffett, Peter Lynch, David Gardner, etc.) almost always **have expectations but never forecast**. They all never profess to know whether the stock market will go up or down in the next day, week, month, or year, but they know it will go up over the long run, and that's all that matters.

Commitment No. 4

We understand that stocks will always **go down faster than they go up**, but stocks will **go up more than they go down** over time.

Market sell-offs present buying opportunities for us, not selling opportunities.

Very Few Winners Will Drive the Majority of Your Entire Portfolio Returns

Dr. Henrik Bessembinder's study "Do Stocks Outperform Treasury Bills?[17]" analyzes data on the U.S. stock market from 1926 to 2016, with stunning revelations. Out of the **25,300 companies** which existed at some point during that time period:

1. **Only 4% — or around 1,000 companies** were **responsible for the entire returns** of the stock market.

---

[17] Hendrik Bessembinder, Do stocks outperform Treasury bills?, Journal of Financial Economics, 2018, vol. 129, issue 3, 440-457 https://www.sciencedirect.com/science/article/abs/pii/S0304405X18301521

2. **Only 0.4%** — or **around 90 companies** were **responsible for more than half of the returns** of the stock market.

3. The remaining **96%, 24,000 companies** had **zero to negative returns**.

These numbers are meant to point out that because **very few companies were responsible for the majority of the market's returns**, it would be difficult for us to find and invest in these companies.

Instead, I prefer we look at the more optimistic side of things rather than to be pessimistic. We are not monkeys throwing darts randomly. If we can apply the right framework to find these winners and own them, our probability of success will be higher.

Commitment No. 5

We commit to find and invest in the best companies for the long-term.

Winners Can Win Big Become Multibaggers and Overwhelm the Losers

Because **mathematically** there is **no limit** as to how much your **winners can go up by** (i.e. >>100% and become multibaggers over time), and the **maximum your losers can go down** is -100%.

Understanding this concept is extremely important.

"Find the winners, invest in them, hold them for the long-term."

The below chart shows that from 1998 through 2017, the median stock returned about 50% cumulatively, which is only a 2.0% annualized return! The average return of the 500 stocks over that time period was 228% cumulatively or 6.1% annualized. Thus, while every stock has a 50/50 chance of being above the median, **each stock has much less than a 50/50 chance of being above average**.

More importantly, it shows how the few winners that are multibaggers drive the majority of the market's returns. Thus, we want to **focus our efforts on a shortlist of a much smaller percentage of the entire investing universe** to **find and invest in the best companies** that are (1) **likely to outperform and beat the market** and (2) the **winners that can become multibaggers**. This is how we flip the odds in our favor and how we look to invest instead.

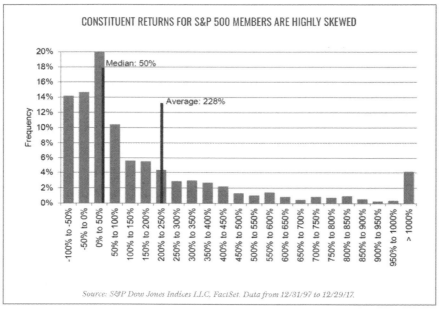

CONSTITUENT RETURNS FOR S&P 500 MEMBERS ARE HIGHLY SKEWED

Source: S&P Dow Jones Indices LLC, FactSet. Data from 12/31/97 to 12/29/17.

Source: The St. Louis Trust Company[18]

1. **You will have very few winners that will drive the majority of your gains and many losers.** But the winners win massively (10X, 100X, 1000X) vs. the losers (-1X), and they take many years to unfold.

2. **There will be losers**, and that is okay. Your portfolio will end up having **much higher returns** because the **massive gains from your winners (>>>>1X) will more than overwhelm the losses from losers** (-100%), as your losers become negligible over time.

---

[18] Source: The St. Louis Trust Company
https://www.stlouistrust.com/why-most-stocks-underperform-index/

Having Multibaggers Will Skew Your Portfolio Returns Positively

Having just 1 multibagger (10X) in Portfolio B **allows the portfolio to significantly outperform and beat the market over time.** If you have a portfolio of 20-50 stocks, all you really need is a handful. **Search, find, invest, and hold these multibaggers**. They are truly the **Holy Grail to investing.**

Portfolio A (with no multibagger)				Portfolio B (with 1 10X multi-bagger)		
No.	Company	% Return		No.	Company	% Return
1	ABC	120%		1	ABC	1000%
2	DEF	100%		2	DEF	100%
3	GHI	90%		3	GHI	90%
4	JKL	-20%		4	JKL	-20%
5	MNO	-40%		5	MNO	-40%
	Average Return	**50%**			**Average Return**	**226%**
	Market Return	50%			Market Return	50%
	Outperformance	**0%**			**Outperformance**	**176%**

Eventually, your portfolio over the long run will look something similar to this[19].

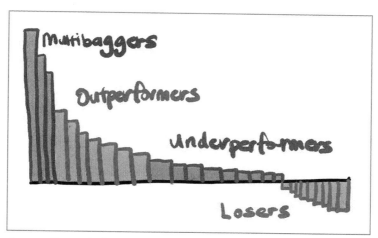

Source: Eugene's drawings

---

[19] My hand-drawn chart. This was drawn in two minutes and provides so much more context than using excel to graph something, though I easily could.

Commitment No. 6

We commit to understanding that the massive gains from a few of our multibagger winners will more than offset the combined losses from our losers as they become negligible over time.

Diversification Is Important Because We Want Winners

3. **You need to have a well-diversified portfolio**, which increases the chances that some of your stocks will become big performers of your buy-and-hold investment strategy. You **need to have at least 15-25 stocks in your portfolio**. Having a small concentrated portfolio of just a few stocks and eventually not having any of the massive outperformers can result in significant underperformance.

Commitment No. 7

We commit to have a diversified portfolio and own at least 15-25 stocks.

QUICK SUMMARY

- Understanding the **math behind investing** is essential to win.
- In the long run, **stocks go up more than they go down**.
- In the short run, **stocks can go down faster than they go up**.
- Use the advantage Wall Street doesn't have: **Invest for the long-term**.
- **Investment expectations** are better than investment forecasts.
- **Multibaggers** will skew your portfolio returns positively. Find them, invest in them, own and hold on to them.

WHY TIME, PATIENCE, AND THE POWER OF COMPOUNDING?

Time and Compounding Are Absolutely Crucial

"It is **time in the markets that matters. Not timing the market.**"

"Time is an investor's best friend.
The variable that has the biggest impact on an
investor's long-term return is the time invested.
*The **longer the time, the greater the compounding of returns.**"*
- Leonard Drago

The **best time to start was yesterday**, but the **next best time is today**. It is **never too late to invest your money.**

I want to share two very important concepts:

The first concept of compounding is heard frequently and is absolutely true:

1. **Holding investments for the long-term and letting it compound over time is the most effective strategy.**

Time and Compounding

Time is truly an investor's best friend. Compound interest is what will make you rich. And it takes time. Warren Buffett is a great investor, but what makes him rich is that he's been a great investor for two-thirds of a century. Of his current **US$83.7 billion net worth (Mar 2018), US$83.3 billion** (99.6% of his wealth) **was added after his 52nd birthday**, and **$76.7 billion** (91.6% of his wealth) **came after his 60th**. If Buffett started saving in his 30s and retired in his 60s, you would have never heard of him. **Buffett's secret is time.** Understand that **the majority of your gain in net worth will come at a much later stage in your investing journey.**

Below is a slightly outdated chart, but it serves visually to bring across the point that at age 83, the majority (~97%) of Buffet's net worth only came after he was 50-years-old.

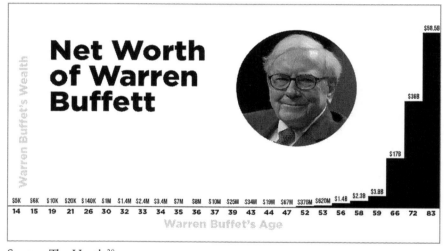

Source: The Hustle[20]

---

[20] Source: The Hustle
https://thehustle.co/how-rich-was-warren-buffet-when-he-was-young

The Rate at Which You Compound Your Investments Matter

Would you like to compound your investments at higher rates of returns or lower rates of returns? **Compounding at 10.5% and 5.0% vs 3.0% yields 4X and 1.5X** of what our capital would have grown to at 3.0% p.a. rates of return.

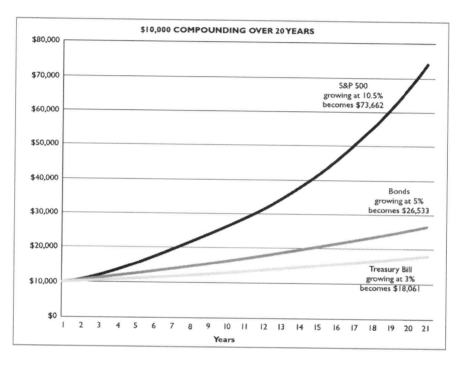

Historic Low-Interest Rates Do Not Help

Both short- and long-term interest rates at all-time historic lows in 500 years.

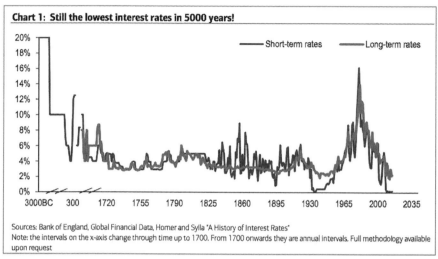

Source: Business Insider Singapore[21]

The **amount of negative-yielding government bonds is at record highs**. One needs to look beyond and build our wealth just investing in bank deposits and fixed income instruments and **earn low single-digit returns** on our investment portfolio.

---

[21] Source: Business Insider Singapore
https://www.businessinsider.sg/5000-year-history-of-interest-rates-2016-12

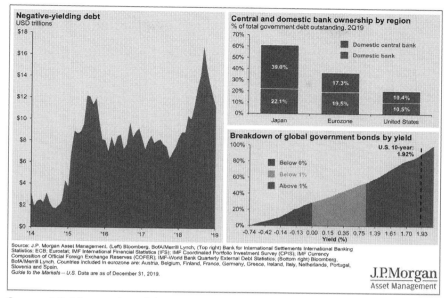

Source: J.P. Morgan Asset Management, Guide to the Markets[22]

---

[22] Source: J.P.Morgan Asset Management, Guide to the Markets
https://am.jpmorgan.com/blobcontent/1383654213584/83456/MI-GT-M_1Q20.pdf

Compounding of Interest on Interest Truly Matters

In compounding, it is the **compounding of interest on interest** that truly yields the largest gains over time.

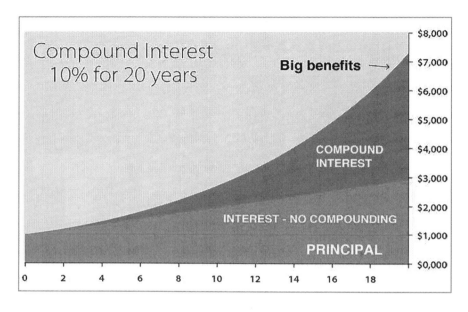

The Arithmetic of Wealth

Understanding the arithmetic of wealth is critical to acquiring wealth. It is your passport to wealth. Arguably, knowing this topic is more important than knowledge about markets.

Income Helps...But Discipline to Save and Invest Matters More

Becoming a millionaire is **not necessarily related to the income you earn**. Innumerable stories can be found about janitors or low-skilled laborers who toiled their entire lives in obscurity. Upon death, these unimportant and unheralded people were discovered to be millionaires or multi-millionaires.

The first one who came up on a Google search — Ronald Read, a janitor and gas station attendant never earned much money but died with an estate of $8 million. His story is not that unusual. There are many more similar stories.

What is common in these cases is a **willingness and discipline to save and invest**. No "keeping up with the Joneses" or pretending you are wealthier than you are. Little if anything is purchased with debt. Lifestyles are sparse. Yet these "nobodies" end up better off than many corporate types who consistently live beyond their means.

These people do not acquire wealth because they have unusual stock market expertise. They **do it with regular savings properly invested**. These surprise millionaires are not Warren Buffets, nor do they have unusual stock expertise or access to inside information. They are **"average Joes"** who do something which today is considered extraordinary—they **live within their means** and **create a nest egg** to protect against the unexpected.

High income is no guarantee for wealth creation. You still need **prudent habits and behavior. Ostentatious spending reflects personal insecurity and also can offset the advantages of high income**, at least for wealth building. If there is one characteristic that tends to identify the "surprise millionaires," it is **humility and self-confidence**. The self-assured end up with wealth beyond what their incomes and lifestyles would suggest. They **live within or below their means**.

The immature and insecure spend what they make (and oftentimes more) to impress and, temporarily, outshine their peers. Whatever produces this insecurity is irrelevant, but it always yields a retirement less comfortable than earnings would suggest.

Building Wealth Is Not about Luck

Becoming a millionaire does not require luck. Millionaires do not depend on wealth creation by winning the lottery to fund their retirement. For every lottery winner, there are millions of losers. For every start-up company that makes it big, there are thousands (perhaps millions) that you never hear about because they fail. **Playing the lottery is not a way to wealth**. Nor is playing the stock market as if it were a lottery.

1. **Delayed Gratification:** When you forgo consuming every penny you earn, you are creating future wealth.
2. **Reduce Borrowings:** Conversely, **borrowing reduces wealth**, at least to the extent that the borrowing is **for consumption** rather than investing. **All credit card debt is wealth reducing**! There is smart leverage and there is stupid leverage; credit card debt is definitely not one of them.
3. **Investing and Compounding:** Investing savings enables it to grow beyond what you saved. Paying interest on credit card debt reduces wealth over and above the amount borrowed.

> *Compounding is "the eighth wonder of the world"*
> *and "the most powerful force in the universe."*
> *- Albert Einstein*

Commitment No. 8

We commit to reduce my borrowings where possible, be disciplined in our spending, save, and invest as much as we possibly can.

A Simple Example of Compound Interest

The future value of your funds depends on **three variables**: (1) the **amount you saved**, (2) **the interest rate you obtained,** and (3) **the period of time you leave the funds in the investment. Higher values** for any of these variables **produce a higher future value** for your funds. Lower variables decrease the future value.

For simplicity, let's work with $100 and an interest rate of 10% per annum. (While this interest rate is high given current conditions, not too long ago you likely would have considered it too low.)

At the end of one year, your hundred dollars will have grown to $110. At the end of the second year, your balance will be $121.0. The extra $1.00 in your account reflects the compounding effect. For year two you earn interest on $110, not $100. You **earn interest on previously earned interest**. This is known as **compounding**.

Table 1: What a one-time $100 savings grows to at different interest rates and over different time periods

The rate of interest you receive and the number of years you leave the $100 invested make large differences in the ending balances after 50 years.

- At **3%** growth, you will have **only $438**.
- But, at **15%,** $100 will have grown to **more than $100,000**.

Therefore, **the rates of return at which you grow your investments matter**. This is not to tell you right now to put all your money into the investments with the highest returns. The purpose is to **raise your awareness** that if you keep compounding investments at low rates of returns, in the near term, you might not be so different from another individual who spends time and allocates more of his/her capital to higher rates of returns. The growth in the latter's investments 20 years and beyond will far exceed that of the former.

ONE TIME INVESTMENT		$100			
Interest Rate / Years	10	20	30	40	50
3.00%	$134	$181	$243	$326	$438
5.00%	$163	$265	$432	$704	$1,147
10.00%	$259	$673	$1,745	$4,526	$11,739
15.00%	$405	$1,637	$6,621	$26,786	$108,366

Using $100 in this table makes it easy to adjust to any other starting figure. Multiples of $100 can be applied to the end numbers to determine their results. For example, if you used $500 as your starting investment, each number in the table would be five times larger than shown. Thus, a one-time $500 investment that earned 15% per year would be worth over $540,000 fifty years in the future.

*Aside: There is a rule of thumb that enables you to approximate these relationships. It is referred to as the **Rule of 72**. It turns out that if you **divide the interest rate into 72**, it provides a reasonable estimate of the **number of years to double your money**. For example, at an interest rate of 3%, it takes about 24 years (i.e. 72 / 3 = 24) for your money to double. At 10% it only takes about 7.2 years (i.e. 72 / 10 = 7.2).*

The above table is not realistic because it does not truly reflect the way people save. That is, people **don't tend to only save once** and then forget it. Most people do (or at least try to) keep saving year after year.

For simplicity, let's **adjust the earlier table one to better reflect continuous savings of $100, not just one time, but every single year.** The new table two below now reflects the value of a $100 annual deposit that continues compounding.

Table Two: What investing $100 each year grows to at different interest rates and over different time periods

INVEST EACH YEAR		$100			
Interest Rate / Years	10	20	30	40	50
3.00%	$1,146	$2,687	$4,758	$7,540	$11,280
5.00%	$1,258	$3,307	$6,644	$12,080	$20,935
10.00%	$1,594	$5,727	$16,449	$44,259	$116,391
15.00%	$2,030	$10,244	$43,475	$177,909	$721,772

The **numbers are larger** because the **savings of $100 occur every year.** One cannot multiply the number of years by the amounts from table one and come up with a correct entry for Table Two. The number is less than that because each subsequent savings has fewer years to earn interest. This illustrates an important point: **Early savings are worth more than later savings.**

The **second table produces significantly larger amounts than** those in the first table. However, they still appear small because the savings assumption is only $100 per year. A more realistic assumption might be that you save $100 per month. A quick approximation of what that would do can be obtained by multiplying the above table accordingly.

Table Three: What investing $1,200 (10x more) each year grows to at different interest rates and over different time periods

The numbers shown in Table Three are beginning to look attractive. The goal of becoming a millionaire now seems in reach, especially for those who have time on their side.

INVEST EACH YEAR		$1,200			
Interest Rate / Years	10	20	30	40	50
3.00%	$13,757	$32,244	$57,090	$90,482	$135,356
5.00%	$15,093	$39,679	$79,727	$144,960	$251,218
10.00%	$19,125	$68,730	$197,393	$531,111	$1,396,690
15.00%	$24,364	$122,932	$521,694	$2,134,908	$8,661,260

Note: multiplying by 12 assumes somewhat overstates the final results. For this table to be correct, $1,200 would have to be deposited each year at the beginning of that year.

The Three Main Key Takeaways:

1) **Start investing as early as you can.** The more you allow your money to compound over time, the better it will be.
2) **Start investing with as much as you can at the beginning and throughout your life.** The more you invest, the more you allow compounding to happen.
3) **Start investing right.** The rates at which your capital and interests compound matters just as much. There is a huge difference

between 3%, 10%, and 15% p.a. Over 30 years, it can amount to ~4X and ~10X for the latter two.

The Price at Which You Bought Was Not Important. How Long You Held It Matters Most.

Below, we have two illustrative examples of Amazon and Netflix which have been extremely strong winners over the last 20 years or so. Does it matter at what price in Jan - Dec 2010 at which we would have bought versus more than 10 years later? Does it matter that you bought higher or lower during the year, month, week, or even intra-day? For the winners that compound massively over time, **whatever price one buys is merely a blip in a long-term chart of a historic upward move higher**.

1. Amazon's $100-185 vs $1,785 last[23]
2. Netflix's $7-30 vs $336 last[24]

Buy in Thirds

If you want to invest in a company that you want to own, you can always buy a little first. You **can always buy in thirds** and subsequent thirds in the future as you see the company grow. **When the company is doing as you expected, and the stock price has gone up**, you know at least you had bought some at a lower price beforehand.

Or instead, if there was a **subsequent market sell-off with no underlying change to the business** when you first invested, it provides you with an even better entry price before and allows you to average your entry price lower.

I **always enter a position via market orders** (because the price intraday to me almost really does not matter), never via lower take-profit entry levels. What happens if I do not get the position and the price moves higher? I

---

[23] Source: YCharts as of 16 March 2020.
[24] Source: YCharts as of 16 March 2020.

do not want to subject myself to such negative emotions of disappointment and be upset. Because whatever **entry prices I get within the day itself almost never matters in the long-term grand scheme of things**. I cannot control how the price is going to move within the day, but what I can control is my own feelings and how I react to it. That's how I manage my own.

Historical Stock Price of Amazon.com Inc (Jan - Dec 2010)

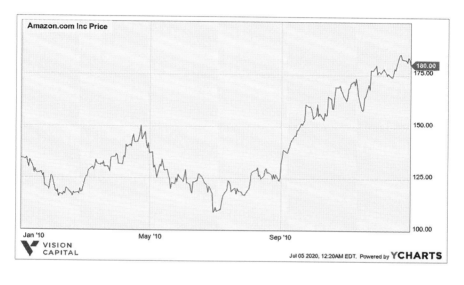

Historical Stock Price of Amazon.com Inc (From Inception)

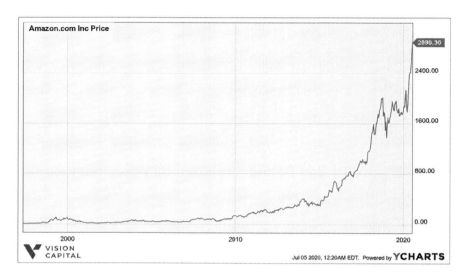

Historical Stock Price of Netflix Inc (Jan - Dec 2010)

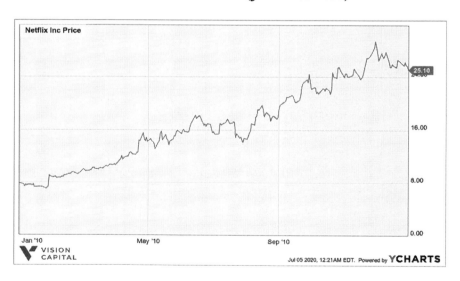

Historical Stock Price of Netflix Inc (From Inception)

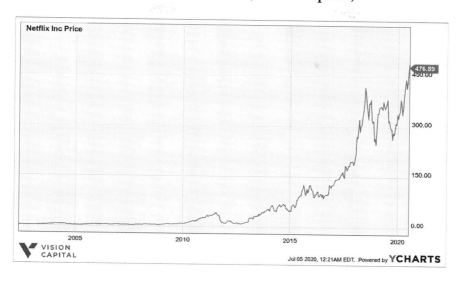

All things said, instead of "If you can't beat 'em, join 'em", we **instead believe "If you can beat 'em, let's go ahead and beat 'em."** This book would just end here if we thought we would not be able to **direct you to better than average returns** in the remaining pages. Now that you know the **power of compounded returns** (remember the concept that the money you make, makes you even more money), you will recognize that every **extra percentage point** that you can raise your investment returns by **will translate to thousands of dollars down the line**. The process can even be relatively painless, even downright fun and agreeable, assuming that you will **enjoy doing some of your own research**, and don't mind **taking on additional risk and responsibility for your own decision making**.

Beating the Market over the Long-Term

The remainder of the book will **concentrate wholly on finding stocks and building investment portfolios that outperform the market average.** You will be surprised at just **how simple and easy** for the **individual investor to top most active mutual fund managers**. The majority of fund managers move from one investment opportunity or theme of the month to another from time to time, follow the herd, underperform the average, keep trimming their winners as they grow larger, and in many cases, end up losing over the long run. It may seem counterintuitive, but **it is true, you have the advantage**.

Aim to exceed 10% average returns over the long-term and beat the market

We want to hammer home again that **we aim to exceed the 10% annual growth the S&P 500 has compounded over the last 100 or so years**. **Beating the S&P 500 over the long-term** should be the goal of every institutional investor in stocks on the planet. Though sadly, for most of them, it is nothing but a dream.

> *"Success in investing doesn't correlate with IQ …*
> *You don't need to be a rocket scientist.*
> *Investing is not a game where the guy with the 160 IQ*
> *beats the guy with 130 IQ."*
> *- Warren Buffett*

QUICK SUMMARY

- **Time** is an investor's **best friend**.
- **Compound interest** matters!
- A high income is no substitute for **lack of discipline** when it comes to investing.
- Do not get hung up on the price you purchased a stock for; **how long you hold it matters more.**
- **Aim to outperform and beat the market** over the long-term.

CHAPTER 7

WHY IS THE RIGHT MINDSET FOR A SUCCESSFUL INVESTOR SO IMPORTANT?

*"The **investor's chief problem**, and even his worst enemy, **is likely to be himself**."*
- Benjamin Graham

*"The **most important quality for an investor is temperament**, not intellect.*
You need a temperament that neither derives great pleasure from being with the crowd or against the crowd."
- Warren Buffett

Why Is the Mindset So Important?

Learning to be patient is one of the most important lessons for investors, but one of the most difficult to internalize. When the market is tanking and your portfolio is down even more with each hit of the refresh key, our natural inclination is to do something.

"You are your own worst enemy." These are the six most important words in investing. Shady financial advisors, incompetent CEOs, and overpriced stocks don't harm your returns even close to the fraction that your own behavior does. That is because **successful investing has far more to do with how you act than with what you know.**

Traits like **good temperament, patience, level-headedness** and the **ability to overcome biases** are more integral to doing well in the market than anything you might learn in a classroom. No matter how much technical knowledge you accumulate or even me telling you the best stocks to buy, the odds are probably higher that you will have an unhappy investing experience. This is unless you understand the behavioral biases we are born with. Because **most investors will continue to buy high, sell low, and earn subpar returns.**

> *"The **biggest investing errors** come **not from factors that are informational or analytical**, but from those that are psychological."*
> — *Howard Marks*

In the following pages, we will cover a number of **psychological cognitive biases** that cause people to do stupid things with their money.

(1) Loss Aversion

When you receive a compliment, you will likely feel good about it for a moment and then it will drift out of your mind. But if someone criticizes you, there's a chance you will be able to recall the details years from now. That is the same with money as well. People **hate losing money more than they like making it.** But this **outsized fear of loss causes us to overreact** and **become too defensive** when the market tumbles, almost always to our detriment. Most **underperformance** is **due to buying high and selling low**, and **loss aversion is almost always the core of that mistake.**

(2) Illusions of Superiority

Most people think they are above average. Conversely, it is often the other way around; investors who have the highest assessment of their skills actually achieve some of the worst performance. This presents two issues: **overconfidence** and no longer wanting to learn because you think you are the best. Both of which will only lead to one's gradual downfall. **Always have humility and stay humble.**

> *"The worst thing you can do is to think that*
> *you are Master of the Universe.*
> *We are nothing and the universe will go on without us."*
> *- Howard Marks*

(3) Aversion to Changing our Minds

We have a natural aversion to changing our minds because that would **imply that our original judgment was wrong.** A lot of this is due to something called "sunk-costs fallacy," not wanting to admit that effort you have already committed to cannot be recovered. The most successful investors have mastered this bias. They can **change their minds with ease and feel no sense of shame.**

(4) Frequency Illusion

Once you notice an event, it seems to keep happening over and over. But often it is not the case. You are no longer oblivious to it, and you end up noticing it more often. For example, the market crash in 2001 and 2008 was so traumatic to investors and the media that they spent the next several years infatuated with the volatile market. In fact, following the crash, market volatility was below average. Investors were simply paying more attention to normal market swings than usual. The most successful investors **always ground themselves with the actual numbers, not their emotions.**

(5) Anchoring Illusion

The market doesn't know, nor does it care what you paid for or what you think a fair price is. Anchoring a price, you paid is one of the most damaging biases investors fall for. Being **able to admit when you are wrong** is key to avoiding this bias. Similarly, if you are holding out to buy a stock as soon as it drops below say $40, you could be missing out on a huge opportunity. It does not make much of a difference whether you bought at $40 or $42 if the stock goes to $200, but if it never drops back to where you wanted to buy, you will be kicking yourself. **If you miss a bump in a stock price while conducting your research, no big deal**. If you **ultimately find a great business to invest in**, that **5% jump** will barely register as a **blip in the long march upward** over a decade or two of that company's dominance, especially when they become multibaggers over time.

(6) Overestimating Self-Control

All investors we know say they will be greedy when others are fearful, but **few actually realize that they are the fearful ones**. By definition, someone has to be. Of course, nobody will say "If stocks fall 20%, I am going to panic and sell." They are far more likely to say that a 20% decline would be a buying opportunity. That's smart, but the **reason there is a 20% crash** is because there is much **more panic selling than opportunistic buying**. That's why investors often overestimate their self-control and they eventually realize that they are the others. **Commit to yourself that your investing horizon is for the long-term, you never sell, you set regular buying opportunities, and reserve some cash for market sell-offs to add to your winners.**

(7) Cognitive Dissonance

Cognitive dissonance is the uncomfortable feeling of holding two contradictory ideas in your head at the same time. "Chocolate brownies are bad for me. I am going to have a chocolate brownie." That's cognitive dissonance, and we are willing to jump through mental hoops to reduce it. The easiest way is to reduce it is to find ways to justify behavior we know is wrong. Investors do it all the time too. You buy a stock only because you think it is cheap and after realizing you were wrong, decide to hold it because you like the company's CEO (or some other reason). **Never underestimate your mind's power to convince you to do something you know you should not. Stick to complete analysis, logical reasoning, and cover both positive factors and negative considerations.**

(8) Normalcy Bias

It is **not common to assume that because something has never happened before, it will not (or cannot) happen in the future.** Everything that has ever occurred in history is always "unprecedented" at one time. The Great Depression. The crash of 1987, 2001, 2008, 2020, Enron, Wall Street Bailouts. None of these events had ever happened... until they did. **Considering all possible downside risks** (where possible) is important because **anything can happen. The only thing we are 100% sure is that the market is volatile and will always continue to be**, nothing else.

(9) Ludic Reasoning

Coined by Nassim Taleb in The Black Swan, this is the **belief that the real world can be predicted with mathematical models and forecasts.** More often than not, the models are purposely simplified, while the real world is incomprehensibly complex. No one can foresee the consequences of trivia and accident, and for that reason alone, the future will always be filled with surprises. **Accepting that some things cannot be predicted or known will help you become a better investor.** We know and recognize that **the market is always a voting machine in the random short-term, full of noise.**

(10) Bandwagon Effect

This is the fallacy of believing something is true because other people think it is. People always like being associated with things that are winning, so winners build momentum— not because they deserve it, but because they are winning. This is the foundation of all asset bubbles. **Have your own opinion and always take full responsibility for your own investing decisions.**

(11) Clustering Illusion

Many investors convince themselves that they found a pattern by taking a small sample out of a much larger one. For example, a gambler will assume a coin is "due" to come up heads after flipping a string of tails, but the outcome of the next flip is completely independent of the previous flip, odds are still 50/50 regardless of prior flips. **Accept that the market is random in the short-term.**

(12) Belief Bias

We tend to accept or reject an argument based on how well it fits our predefined beliefs, rather than the objective facts of the situation. When presented with information that goes against our point of view, we **not only reject challenges** but also **double down on our original view** only because the topic becomes more emotional. We tend to stick our heads under a pillow when confronted with information that makes us uncomfortable. We check our brokerage accounts less frequently when the market is down and ignore dire warnings when we are bullish on a company. **Our ability to ignore things we do not want to believe are true is much stronger than our desire to know the truth.**

(13) Bias Bias

Finally, the most important and powerful bias of them all, "**bias bias.**" It is the **belief that you are less biased than you really are** and more importantly **you can be as biased as everyone else. Know that you can be biased, and you need to know when you are.**

Is That All?

We have clearly run through enough biases and fallacies to keep your head spinning. There are literally hundreds more if not thousands in many shapes and forms we have not discussed. Hopefully, by running through this list, we have made you more aware of some of the most common detriments to ourselves.

Most importantly, the underlying theme remains, "**You are your own worst enemy in Investing**". You can attempt to become smarter investors by learning more about balance sheets, income statements, valuation models, and other textbook finance techniques. That's all useful until we really understand how our brain works against us to misinterpret, abuse, and ignore that knowledge.

The world's best investors know finance inside and out. But the **skills that set them apart** are **control over their emotions, the ability to think clearly under stress, the ability to avoid temptation**, and the understanding of the biases and fallacies that we often ignore. **Everyone is prone to cognitive errors, some more than others**, but no one is exempt, not even the world's top investors.

Coming to terms with the idea with **humility** that you are your own worst enemy is the single most important thing you can do to become a better investor. Because even if you have the best tools to identify the best companies to invest, if you cannot manage your own temperament and emotions well and keep doing the wrong things—panic and sell when the market sells off, or sell when the market is good only to have the stock keep rising, you can end up performing badly still.

We cannot emphasize how important this is. Hence, we look to provide you with some principles towards the end of the book that you can follow to keep you on track and your emotions separate.

QUICK SUMMARY

- **Patience** leads to wealth creation.
- Mindset can **make or break** an investor.
- Understand your **psychological cognitive biases**.
- It is **futile to fight against these biases. Use principles and commitments instead** to manage how you react to them.

PART II
PICKING WINNERS

CHAPTER 8

WHAT ARE THE TYPES OF COMPANIES AND QUALITIES THAT WE LOOK FOR?

Why Buy Blue Chips?

You can find good ideas for investments within your own industry, interests, insight, and investigation. In fact, there are in excess of 40,000 listed companies in the world[25]; the World Bank estimates 43,342 in 2018 alone. How do we determine whether any of these companies are good businesses that we should be analyzing further and investing in?

First, it is useful to classify these investments to get a sense of the level of risk each entails. Any company of any size can rise or fall precipitously in any given year, month, week, or day.

What Are Blue-Chip Companies?

IBM, Walmart, AT&T, and JP Morgan Chase. What do all of these companies have in common? Despite the fact that they are all in different industries, they are each known as a "blue-chip" company.

---

[25] Source: World Bank
https://data.worldbank.org/indicator/CM.MKT.LDOM.NO

Blue-chip companies[26] or "blue-chips" tend to have **higher market cap-italization**, are **well-known, well-established, and well-capitalized.** Such companies are considered to be the **established leaders** in their re-spective sectors or industries and produce dominant goods or services. They tend to be **mature and profitable**, perceived as **safe, stable, long-lasting** and **relatively impervious to economic downturns**, which contributes to their quality of being able to generate consistent revenues and sustain stable growth over time. They're also often considered a household name. Thus, seen as **relatively safe, low volatility investments.**

Quick Note on Market Capitalization

Market capitalization refers to the **total dollar market value of a com-pany's outstanding shares of stock.** Commonly referred to as "market cap," it is calculated by multiplying the total number of a company's out-standing shares by the current market price of one share. As an example, a company with 10 million shares selling for $100 each would have a market cap of $1 billion. Market Cap is one of the best measures of a company's size, as opposed to using sales or total asset figures.

We typically divide the market cap of companies **into four categories**:

1. **Large-cap** ($10 billion or more)
2. **Mid-cap** ($2 billion to $10 billion)
3. **Small-cap** ($300 million to $2 billion)
4. **Micro-cap** (less than $300 million)

Note: everyone has their own definition of these categories, but these numbers represent a dependable enough guide. Note that these numbers can vary from one country to another and might be higher as companies start becoming larger.

---

[26] The term "blue-chip" originates from the game of high-stakes poker where different coloured gambling chips representing different dollar values are used and the color blue signifies the chip with the highest value on the table,

Quick One on Each

Large-cap companies typically have a market capitalization of $10 billion or more. These large companies have usually been around for a long time, and they are **major players in well-established industries**. Investing in large-cap companies does not necessarily bring in huge returns in a short period of time, but **over the long run**, these companies **generally reward investors with a consistent increase in share value and dividend payments**.

Mid-cap companies generally have a market capitalization of between $2 billion and $10 billion. Mid-cap companies are **established companies** that operate in an industry **expected to experience rapid growth**. Mid-cap companies are in the process of expanding. They **carry an inherently higher risk** than large-cap companies because they are **not as established**, but they are **attractive for their growth potential**.

Small-cap companies generally have a market capitalization of between $300 million to $2 billion. These small companies **could be young in age and/or they could serve niche markets and new industries**. These companies are **considered higher risk** investments due to their **age, the markets they serve, and their size**. Smaller companies with fewer resources are more sensitive to economic slowdowns.

Why Invest in Blue-chip Companies?

The Dow Jones Industrial Average (DJIA) and S&P 500 contain some of the largest corporations on the planet. The DJIA is a price-weighted index comprising the shares of 30 large public US companies (versus the S&P 500 is market-weighted).

Why would you invest in one of these giants? **To outperform.**

There is no reason not to invest in any specific stocks **unless you believe by doing so, you can outdo** the boring 10% in compounded growth in an index fund or ETF over the long-term. It is risky to trade speculative stocks, bonds, futures, commodities, gold coins, options, CFDs, or hop on any cool-sounding indecipherable Big New Thing that sounds too good to be true. The unfortunate thing is that so many greenhorn investors still make unstudied rolls each year. If you jump in with a risky approach and limited understanding, it is not investing. It is gambling...not too different from rolling a dice in a casino...and an excellent long-term approach to losing money (remember the house always wins?).

Remember in Chapter 5 (see below) of all the 24,000 companies analyzed:

1. **Only 4%, ~ 1,000 companies** were **responsible for the majority of the returns**
2. **Only 0.4%, ~ 90 companies** were **responsible for more than 50% of returns**

Thus, what we are trying to do is to **find and invest in the best companies** (from more than 40,000 available) **that are most likely to outperform** (the 0.4%, if not the 4%!) and **beat the market in the process.**

The second reason to invest in large-cap companies is that you end up working from a **smaller sample of potential investments.** One of the greatest mistakes individual investors make is trying to follow too many stocks. NYSE and NASDAQ combined have over 6,000 stocks. It can be tempting to fire up your favorite financial website and say, "I will conquer you all." But it ain't gonna happen.

Investors who try to manage too much research typically run unprofitable or underperforming portfolios. It may help you sleep better at night to start by **staying on top of only a few stable stocks, selected from five hundred of the strongest, most profitable, and most immense companies in the world.** Now isn't that better?

That's not to say that blue-chips are completely safe. Many companies have risen and similarly fallen with time in both the S&P 500 and DJIA. General Electric was the last remaining of the 1916 original DJIA list and was removed in 2018. A look at the following two tables will show how components of the DJIA have evolved over time.

Continuous monitoring (over quarters and years) **is needed to see if the business is deteriorating. Even the blue-chips need watching.**

June 26, 2018 [edit]

3M Company	The Goldman Sachs Group, Inc.	Pfizer Inc.
American Express Company	The Home Depot, Inc.	The Procter & Gamble Company
Apple Inc.	Intel Corporation	The Travelers Companies, Inc.
The Boeing Company	International Business Machines Corporation	UnitedHealth Group Inc.
Caterpillar Inc.	Johnson & Johnson	United Technologies Corporation
Chevron Corporation	JPMorgan Chase & Co.	Verizon Communications, Inc.
Cisco Systems, Inc.	McDonald's Corporation	Visa Inc.
The Coca-Cola Company	Merck & Co., Inc.	Walgreens Boots Alliance, Inc. ↑
DowDuPont Inc.	Microsoft Corporation	Walmart Inc.
Exxon Mobil Corporation	Nike, Inc.	The Walt Disney Company
Dropped from Average		
General Electric Company ↓		

General Electric was replaced by Walgreens Boots Alliance.

October 4, 1916 [edit]

The American Beet Sugar ↑ [5]	Anaconda Copper Mining Company	The Texas Company ↑
American Can Company ↑	The Baldwin Locomotive Works ↑	United States Rubber Company
American Car and Foundry Company	Central Leather Company	United States Steel Corporation
American Locomotive Company ↑	General Electric Company	Utah Copper Company ↑
American Smelting & Refining Company	B.F. Goodrich Corporation ↑	Western Union Company ↑
The American Sugar Refining Company	Republic Iron and Steel Company ↑	Westinghouse Electric Corporation ↑
American Telephone and Telegraph Company ↑	Studebaker Corporation ↑	
Dropped from Average		
General Motors Corporation ↓	National Lead Company ↓	Peoples Gas Light and Coke Company ↓
United States Steel Corporation (Preferred) ↓		

The index was expanded to twenty companies.
General Motors, National Lead, Peoples Gas and U.S. Steel (Preferred) were removed.
American Beet Sugar, American Can, American Locomotive, AT&T, Baldwin Locomotive, Goodrich, Republic Iron, Studebaker, Texas Company, Utah Copper, Western Union, Westinghouse Electric were added.

Source: Wikipedia[27]

---

[27] Source: Wikipedia - Historical components of the Dow Jones Industrial Average https://en.wikipedia.org/wiki/Historical_components_of_the_Dow_Jones_Industrial_Average

Why Small-Cap Stocks?

(1) Small numbers can multiply much more rapidly than big ones

Small-cap stocks make an attractive addition to an investment portfolio in addition to the world's blue chips. It is not hard to figure out why. Because it is **far easier for a small-cap** $1 billion market cap company **to grow 10X to $10 billion off a smaller base**, compared to a **large-cap** $500 billion market cap company **to grow 10X** to $5 trillion **off a larger base**.

(2) Small-caps have historically produced excellent returns

There are many studies and **depending on the study** you look at and the time frame, **small-caps either outperform or they don't.** Provided below is an example, which they do. More importantly, **either way, we think small-caps make a great addition to a well-diversified portfolio.**

Source: Small-cap Asia[28]

---

[28] Source: Small-cap Asia
https://www.smallcapasia.com/3-big-reasons-to-invest-in-small-cap-stocks/
small-cap-outperform-large-caps-historically/

(3) Small-caps are typically underinvested by fund managers

That's a space that as individual investors, we can play. In addition, many fund managers just by pure size **cannot own or invest in many small-caps yet**. Or even if they can, **they can't build up any meaningful holding**. Meaningful here is defined as "in a sufficient quantity to make any noticeable difference to the fund's overall performance."

Just imagine a $10 billion AUM fund allocating 1% of their capital of $100mil in a 10% holding in a small-cap that has a $1 billion market cap. Because **any serious attempt by any fund to establish a meaningful stake** would often involve owning a huge chunk of these companies, they will **push up the price so quickly** that their entry prices would be beyond the initial attractive entry point. Also, when it comes time to sell a big stake, **prices can be equally driven down as far and fast as it was driven up**.

The best buy of all is the purchase of a small-cap before the institutional fund managers "discover" it. By concentrating a portion of your portfolio in **excellent small companies**, **you give yourself a great shot at beating mutual funds by a wide margin.**

(4) Earnings grow fastest among small companies

And what often accompanies earnings growth is share price growth. That was done most convincingly by Peter Lynch in his wonderful book, *One Up on Wall Street*. He made a whole career focusing on growth stocks and generating superior returns in the process. Often these high growth small-caps are also more expensive by traditional valuation metrics with a lot of future growth priced into the existing share price. Thus, closer attention has to be placed with respect to business quality and potential.

(5) Small-caps are typically owned by management

Another reason to like small-caps is that they are typically closely held by management. Incentives are aligned and management is focused on the long-term success rather than the short-term. Because the people running the company have a significant financial stake in the success, not just of the company, but also of the stock itself. In fact, in many cases, the performance of the stock has a greater influence on the wealth of the management team than their annual salaries and more likely account for the majority of their wealth as well.

(6) Small-caps are also more likely to be founder-owned and led

Typically, they are paid much less in cash versus stock options that vest over the long term (3-5 years), which means they have to be long-term focused as their future is tied closely to the success of the business. They are making a bet on themselves. Their goals are aligned with the goals of outside investors like us. And that can be a very good place to be for early investors in a company, as it begins its long and steady march higher up to be a bigger company with time.

Avoid Small-Caps If You Don't Have Time or Are Unwilling to Follow Them

You definitely should not buy small-caps if you don't know what you are doing. Small-caps **need to be paid more attention** to than large-caps because they are subject to a larger impact from any major risks than a large-cap. Also, **never ever plunge because you got a "hot tip." Always do your homework before and after you invest in small-caps**.

Taking on Smart Risks

We believe in taking on **smart risk** and **understand and appreciate** the value of strong small-cap appreciation. **Embrace risk** because the opposite is timidity. Remember fortune favors the bold. **Handled properly**, small-cap investing can be **tremendously fun and exceptionally lucrative**. But **small-caps should not be your first and definitely not your only type of stocks you own**. We **always recommend balance** in your investing (not to mention your life as well, but that's another book).

How Then Do We Find the Best Stocks?

*"If you **don't study** any companies,*
*you have the **same success** buying stocks as you do*
*in a poker game if you **bet without looking at your cards**."*
- Peter Lynch

By now, you have hopefully come to understand that whether you are **pursuing small-caps or blue chips or something in between, investing can be fun and rewarding**, opening up a world of opportunities for you and the life-changing wealth you have accumulated through smart decisions and savvy insights.

The difference is largely in the specific investments you make. With so many companies publicly traded in the United States and around the globe, how do you determine which stocks to buy? There are as many answers to that question as there are stocks in the market.

Some people rely on fancy-looking charts and graphs that show the very lowest a stock can go and buy them, right until it goes even lower. Others follow the advice of TV talking heads (e.g. CNBC, Bloomberg, etc.) who we must remember are focused more on ratings than returns.

As you start to appreciate by now, we **embrace a long-term buy and hold strategy** that **focuses on finding great businesses** and **investing in them for years and even decades**. In particular, we **recommend "business-focused investing,"** by seeking out **great and amazing growth opportunity businesses rather than rely on a mechanical formula.** We ask ourselves **where the company,** not the stock, **will be in the next three to five years and beyond.** We look at **criteria** such as **competitive advantage, market opportunity, strength of leadership, and other characteristics** that are tough to push into a financial calculator or spreadsheet.

Don't get us wrong, there is value in **uncovering and understanding a company's financials**...we will get to that in the next few chapters, then we will take a look at the **criteria** we use **to help us find these great companies.**

We should be **approaching investing with a "business owner" mentality rather than a "stock buyer" one**. (E.g. I own Apple Inc, rather than I am currently long or just bought Apple or AAPL).

The "Snap" Test

The **"Snap Test"** was introduced to me by David Gardner.

What if you had the **power to snap your fingers and make any public company disappear?**

For instance, **social media**. Whether the platform is Facebook, Instagram, or WhatsApp. Snap. It's gone. Or maybe for a lot of us, **Netflix**, our favorite video entertainment. Snap, and it's gone. Or, even more consequentially, what about **Amazon.com**? Don't do it! Snap. Gone. Or how about **Visa** and **Mastercard** which we use to pay for almost everything? **Spotify** for all my music? **Google** Search and Maps or YouTube? Hopefully, you get the drift by now.

The Snap Test **asks you as an investor, if you snapped your fingers** (think Thanos snapping his fingers in The Avengers) and **a company disappeared, would anyone notice? Would anyone care? Would society and the world truly miss it?**

Companies that pass the Snap Test, we feel almost everyone would notice, and lots of people would care. It's one of the surest signs to a winning stock.

In fact, I would challenge you to write down a list of the companies whose products you use day in and day out and look at the companies from there. It is usually a great place to start.

QUICK SUMMARY

- **Blue-chip** companies can produce solid returns. They are well-known, well-established, and well-capitalized.
- Small-cap stocks can produce even much higher **returns** over time.
- Always apply **the "Snap Test"** to your investments.

CHAPTER 9

WHAT DO WE LOOK FOR IN A COMPANY'S FINANCIAL STATEMENTS?

As we go through the following financial terms quite a lot, you will need to **understand accounting and financial metrics** to **determine how a business is doing**. These tools are crucial as to how you can determine if a business is good, whether the current price makes sense and whether you want to own this business for the long run.

Earnings Drive Share Prices

But remember, ultimately it is **earnings** that **drive the long-term share price of a company**, and that is what we want you to remember as we dive into the following chapters.

> "In the **short run**, the market is a **voting machine**
> but in the **long run**, the market is a **weighing machine**."
> - Benjamin Graham

Earnings Drive Long-Term Stock Prices

The following chart compares the S&P 500 index with its trailing twelve-month (TTM) earnings per share (EPS) value back to 1935. As you can see, the S&P 500 always moves higher along with earnings, but at times, the S&P 500 may rise higher (massive rallies) and may decline much lower (during market selloffs). Always remember, **the market is a weighing machine in the long run, not a voting machine.** In the short run, market prices can be higher or it can be lower.

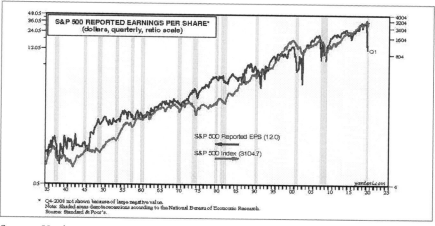

Source: Yardeni Research (Jun 2020)

S&P 500 and Earnings – What do they tell us?

The following 5 historical charts compare the S&P 500 index with its trailing 12-month (TTM) earnings per share (EPS) from 1926, over the last 30, 20, 10, and 5 years. Shaded areas are when economic recessions occurred.

Though sometimes, stock prices can move up faster than the rise in earnings and vice versa, where stock prices can move down faster than the decline in earnings.

What should be extremely clear is that **earnings almost always drive the long-term rise in stock prices**. And this is clearly evident across all long-term time horizons.

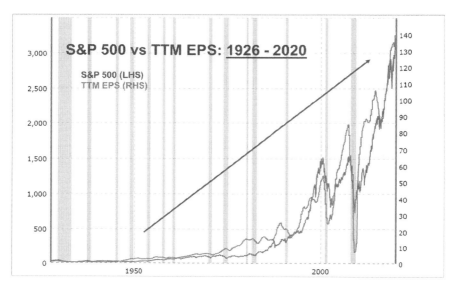

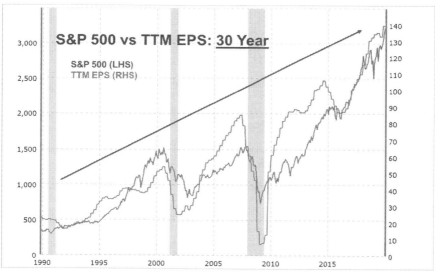

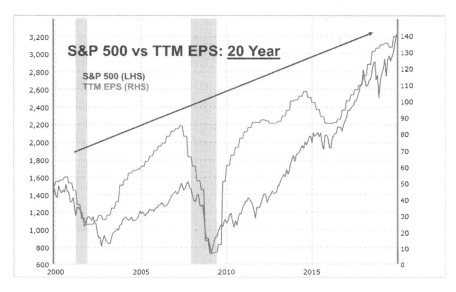

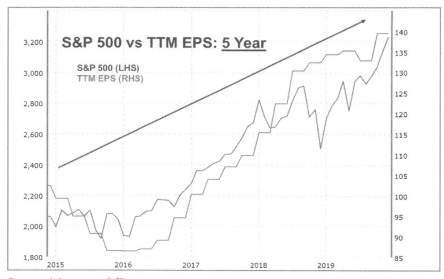

Source: Macrotrends[29]

What is key to realize in the next chart is that the **market can assign different price tags at each time, as PE ratios can vary throughout time**. Sometimes it can really get out of whack like in the 2000 dot com bubble crash (almost 50 times) and the 2008 financial crisis (120 times). Looking at the last 30 years, the **long-term average PE of the S&P 500 would be around 10-25 times**. Anything higher, we need to ask ourselves if we are expecting a sudden earnings growth that is not yet reflected in the trailing 12 months earnings that we are using. If not, it could be likely that the market is ahead of itself and that prices should be overbought and are looking too optimistic and overvalued versus the fundamentals. Conversely, if the PE of the S&P trades lower than the long-term average, it could likely mean that the market is overly pessimistic and undervalued compared to fundamentals.

---

[29] Source: Macrotrends
https://www.macrotrends.net/1324/s-p-500-earnings-history

Market Valuations Will Vary throughout Time

The following chart shows the trailing 12-month S&P 500 PE ratio or price-to-earnings ratio back to 1926.

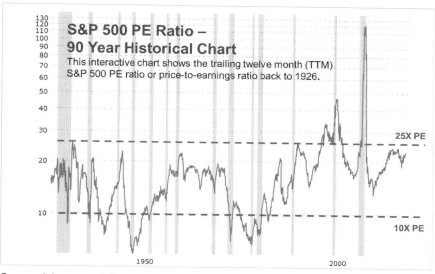

Source: Macrotrends[30]

---

[30] Source: Macrotrends (1950 - 28 March 2020)
https://www.macrotrends.net/2577/sp-500-pe-ratio-price-to-earnings-chart

Below is another example where S&P 500 trades **relative to the implied levels** based on **different PE ratios** (10x, 15x, 20x and 25x) **versus forward earnings**.

Source: Yardeni Research[31]

If earnings of companies (i.e. EPS) drive how the equity index performs over time, surely it must be as well for individual equities, as we shall see in the following charts.

---

[31] Source: Yardeni Research (in June 2020)
https://www.yardeni.com/pub/peacockblueangel.pdf

Below are three examples of companies, **Berkshire Hathaway Inc, J.P. Morgan Chase & Co,** and **Amazon Inc**, where **long-term earnings growth** eventually **drives the move higher in their respective stock prices**.

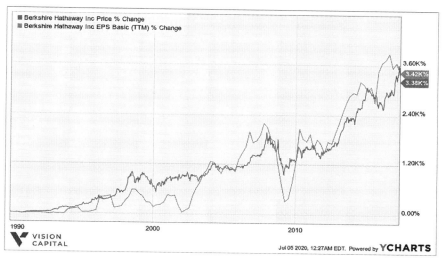

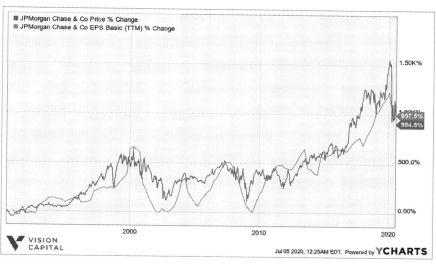

Suddenly Amazon's stock price increase does not seem that ridiculous, because it is driven by earnings growth...

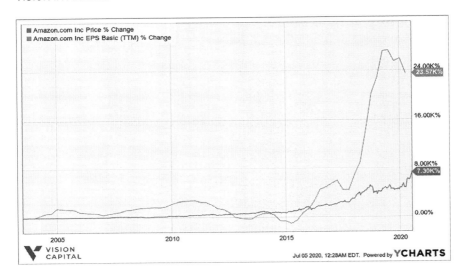

Below are three examples of companies, **General Electric & Co, Under Armour Inc,** and **Sears Holdings Co** where **long-term decline in earnings** eventually **drove the move lower in their respective stock prices lower over time.**

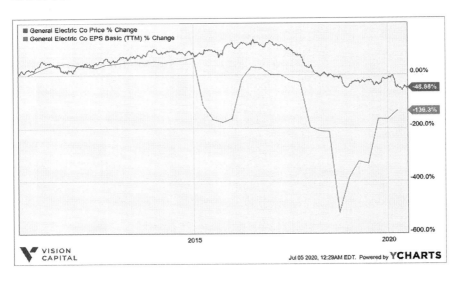

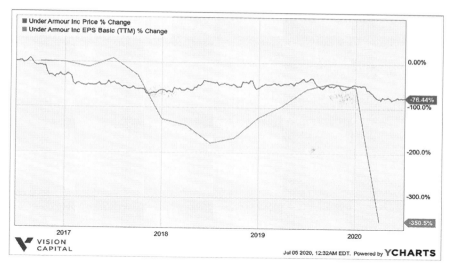

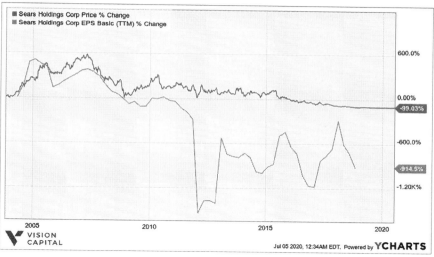

We can share more of these charts to bring across the point, but this is merely to give you a flavor of what **you should** ultimately **be looking for in a business: <u>Earnings</u>**.

We **like companies that are profitable and are growing to become even more profitable** because eventually, these companies will grow in value. Likewise, we **do not like companies that are not profitable and are struggling to return to profitability**.

Nonetheless, we can potentially like **investing in companies that might not be profitable now** but are **growing rapidly** and **already showing signs of improving profitability** with the **path to profitability becoming clear with time**.

Revenues will ultimately drive earnings. If revenues don't grow, there is a limit as to how much earnings can really grow. The disconnect almost never lasts.

Nonetheless, there are a lot of moving parts in between revenues leading to earnings. So, let's get there and try to arm ourselves with the tools to understand how a business works.

Financial Statements

Publicly traded companies must produce the following three statements for each quarter and each year in accordance with GAAP (US) or IFRS (rest of the world) principles.

1) **Income Statement**
2) **Balance Sheet**
3) **Cash Flow Statement**

(1) Income Statement

The income statement is one of three financial statements that stock investors need to become familiar with (the other two are balance sheet and cash flow statement). The income statement is a report that **measures a company's financial performance over a specific accounting period**. This statement is also known by a number of other names: profit & loss statement or earning statement. Publicly traded companies must produce income statements, balance sheets, and cash flow statements for each quarter and each year in accordance with GAAP or IFRS principles.

The income statement shows a company's **revenue, expenses, and profits** from both operating and non-operating activities. It lists the company's:

1. **Net Sales**
2. **Cost of Goods / Sales** (COGS)
3. **Gross Income / Profit**

In addition, after Gross Profit, it further breaks down into three main expenses:

1. **Sales & Marketing** expenses (S&M)
2. **General and Administrative** expenses (G&A)
3. **Research & Development** expenses (R&D)

It can also include other items like:

1. **Other Income / Expenses** (tend to be non-operating)
2. **Special / Extraordinary items** (tend to be one-off)

Thus, revealing the profitability of a company with:

1. **Gross Profit**
2. **Operating Profit** (EBIT)
3. **EBITDA** (EBIT less depreciation & amortization)
4. **Pretax Profit** (EBT)
5. **Net Income** (After Tax Profit)

The income statement splits into two parts:

1) **Operating** Sections (directly related to business)
2) **Non-Operating** Sections

Understanding an income statement is essential for investors in order to **analyze the profitability** and **future growth of a company**, which should play a huge role in deciding whether or not to invest in it.

We are ultimately looking for these three things, but not only from an **absolute increase, the YoY growth** (YoY % increase), and the **trend of the growth** (if the growth is declining and at how fast):

1. **Increasing Revenues**
2. **Expenses increasing at a decreasing rate** (vs revenues)
3. **Increasing Profits**

The **less money a company has to spend** on every single dollar it earns (lower expenses), **the more money it earns** (higher revenues), **the more profitable it is** (higher profits). These are the companies we especially like to own.

The **Three Income Statement Formulas** you must definitely know:

1. **Revenue** - Cost of Goods = **Gross Profit**
2. **Gross Profit** - S&M - G&A - R&D = **Operating Profit / EBIT**
3. **EBIT** - Interest - Taxes = **Net Income**

Specifically, we focus not just on the absolute numbers, but the rate of growth or decline, the margins, and whether they are improving. The following tables indicate specifically what we do like.

Income Statement Item		What We Like
Revenue	↑	1. **Rapid YOY Growth Rates** 2. **Recurring & if rising percentage** 3. **Net Dollar Based Retention Rates**
(Cost of Goods)	↓↓	1. **Rising slower than Revenues** 2. **Improving & declining margins**
Gross Profit	↑↑	1. **Growing faster than Revenues** 2. **Improving & rising margins**

(Sales & Marketing Expenses)	↓↓	1. Rising slower than Revenues 2. Declining as % of sales
(General & Admin Expenses)	↓↓	1. Rising slower than Revenues 2. Declining as % of sales
(R&D Expenses)	↓↓	1. Rising slower than Revenues 2. Declining as % of sales
Operating Profit / EBIT	↑↑↑	1. Growing faster than Revenues 2. Improving & rising margins
Net Income	↑↑↑↑	1. Growing faster than Revenues 2. Improving & rising margins

Why Operating Leverage Is Something We Look for

One measure that often does not get enough attention is **operating leverage**, which **captures the relationship between a company's fixed and variable costs**. Operating leverage is something that we prefer that businesses we own have. And if the business model has truly almost infinite operating leverage as it grows, this will drive multi-year profit growth and would likely lead to massive share price gains over time.

In good times, **operating leverage can supercharge profit growth**. In bad times, it can crush profits. But we are looking for growing companies, not struggling companies.

Essentially, operating leverage boils down to an analysis of fixed costs and variable costs. **Operating leverage is highest** in companies that have a **high proportion of fixed operating costs in relation to variable operating costs** (at least at the beginning). As the company sells more, the higher revenues can be divided by the same fixed costs, and the fixed costs as a percentage of revenues decline and the increase in revenues flow straight through to the bottom line via profits.

The benefits of high operating leverage can be immense. **Companies with high operating leverage can make more money from each additional sale if they don't have to increase costs to produce more sales**. The minute business picks up, fixed assets such as property, plant, and equipment (PP&E), as well as existing workers, can do a whole lot more without adding additional expenses. Profit margins expand and earnings soar faster.

Real-Life Examples of Operating Leverage

The best way to explain operating leverage is by way of example. Take, for example, a software maker such as **Microsoft**. The **bulk of this company's cost structure is fixed and limited to upfront development and marketing costs**. Whether it sells one copy or 10 million copies of its latest Windows software, Microsoft's costs remain basically unchanged. So once the company has sold enough copies to cover its fixed costs, **every additional dollar of sales revenue drops into the bottom line**. In other words, Microsoft possesses remarkably high operating leverage.

By contrast, a **retailer such as Wal-Mart demonstrates relatively low operating leverage**. The company has **fairly low levels of fixed costs**, while its **variable costs are large**. Merchandise inventory represents Wal-Mart's biggest cost. For each product sale that Wal-Mart rings in, the company has to pay for the supply of that product. As a result, Wal-Mart's cost of goods sold (COGS) continues to rise as sales revenues rise.

One can argue that if the company goes into a downturn, high operating leverage can be the company's Achilles' Heel. But what we are **truly looking out for** is not intra-year but long-term **multi-year operating leverage** that a company has, as **revenues grow 5X, 10X, 20X, 50X. Profits soar even faster 10X, 50X, 100X, 200X,** and what will follow, slowly but **surely, the stock price will move higher** as well.

Point to note, operating leverage can exist in various combinations in our opinion and could be a combination of any of the following 4 expenses:

1. **Cost of Goods / Sales** (COGS)
2. **Sales & Marketing** expenses (S&M)
3. **General and Administrative** expenses (G&A)
4. **Research & Development** expenses (R&D)

To illustrate my example, let us look at the following three five-year charts of **Universal Display Corporation (NASDAQ: OLED),** who is the leader in the OLED technologies and materials for use in display and solid-state lighting applications. Looking at the first chart, in absolute terms, profits (gross profit, EBITDA, EBIT & net income) have increased as revenues grow along with time. But when we look at the second chart, in relative terms, because of operating leverage, profits (+120-230%) end up growing faster than revenues (+112%). One should not be surprised to see this company outperform the S&P 500 over time, and indeed it has over the last 10 years, returning more than 6X vs the S&P 500.

OLED: Revenues & Profits Increased in Absolute Numbers with Time

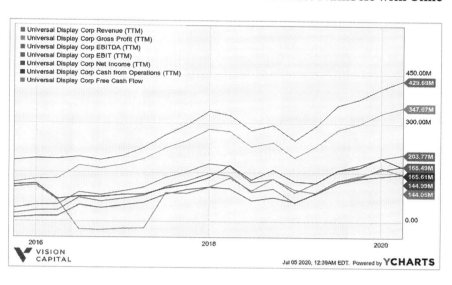

OLED: Growth in Profits Exceed That of Revenues

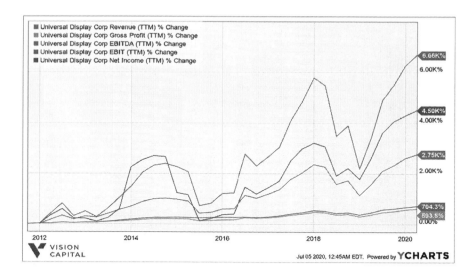

OLED: Outperformance vs S&P 500

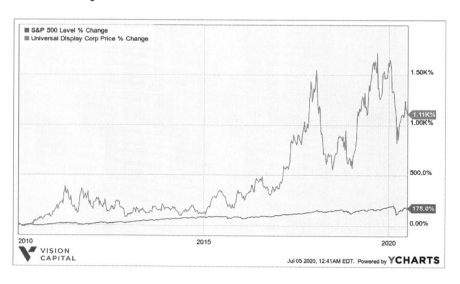

Providing another example of **Microsoft Corporation** (NASDAQ: MSFT) with the following three charts over 30 years. The story again does not differ too much. **Profits grew so much faster than revenues over time**, but look at how much **net income (+18,000%)** and EBITDA

(+14,500%) grew vs **revenues (+12,500%)**. No surprise, Microsoft has outperformed the S&P 500 by more than 25X, MSFT (+33,370%) vs S&P 500 (+1290%).

MSFT: Revenues & Profits Increased in Absolute Numbers with Time

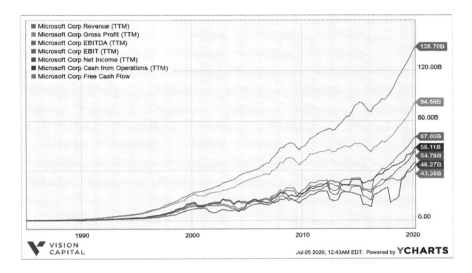

MSFT: Growth in Profits Exceed That of Revenues

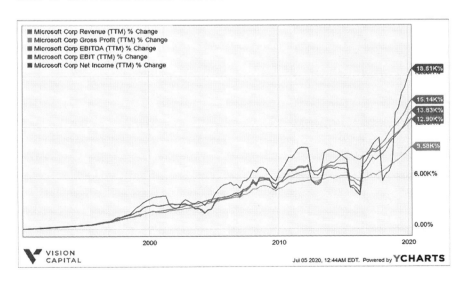

MSFT: Outperformance vs S&P 500

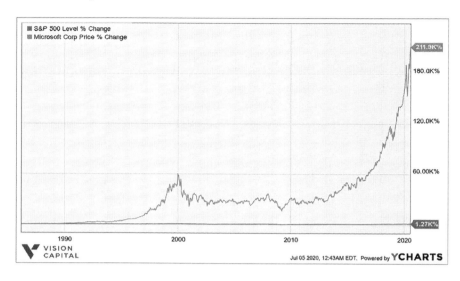

We can give you so many examples, but let me give you one last one for the road.

Let's look at **Apple Inc. (NASDAQ: AAPL).** Apple designs, develops, and sells consumer electronics including some of our beloved Apple products (Mac, iPhone, iPad, iPods, Apple Watch, Air Pods, Apple TV, etc.). Note that the word "manufacture" is missing from the above description; that's absolutely right because Apple does not manufacture a single hardware product. Instead, Apple outsources the manufacturing of all (if not most) of its hardware products to contract manufacturers that are located primarily in Asia, with some Mac computers manufactured in the U.S. and Ireland. Again, **Apple's growth in net income (+10,600%) more than doubled that of revenues (+4690%),** and you should not be surprised to see **Apple's share price outperform the S&P 500**, which indeed Apple has **(+15000% vs +1290%)** since inception.

"Earnings (almost) always drive share price gains over the long term."[32]
- Eugene Ng

AAPL: Revenues & Profits Increased in Absolute Numbers with Time

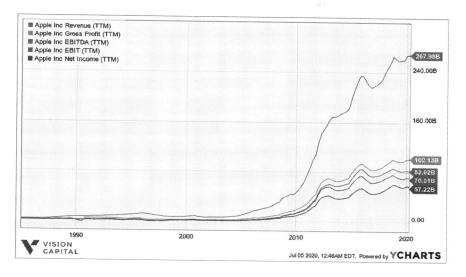

AAPL: Growth in Profits Exceed That of Revenues

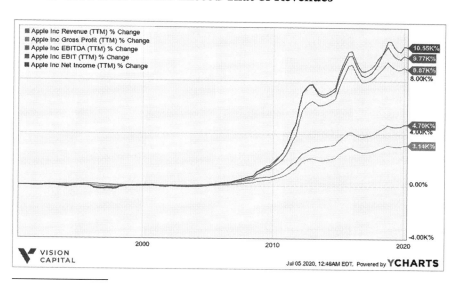

---

[32] I have yet to find one that does not. And if you do, please share it with me. My only precondition, it has to be at least over 5 years because long-term is the only term that really counts.

AAPL: Outperformance vs S&P 500

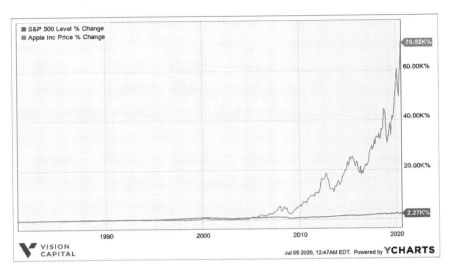

Companies are always and eventually valued based on how many dollars they actually make (i.e. **earnings**) and a valuation multiple of that. If we can **find and invest in fast-growing companies that can be massively profitable with time**, we would have further increased our likelihood of success. We especially **avoid companies which are unprofitable and become even more unprofitable as they grow**, because that is not eternally sustainable.

Profit Margins

We **prefer to own companies** with (1) **stable and consistent profit margins** or (2) **companies that might not be profitable now** but **have demonstrated some form of improving profitability** (less negative margins) and are looking to **move towards a clear path to profitability** (rising positive margins).

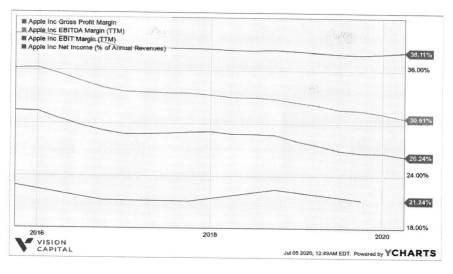

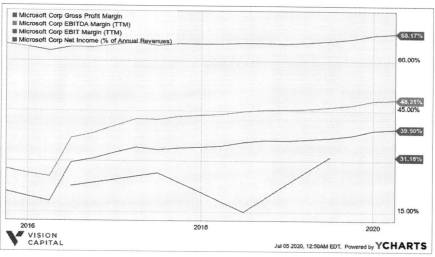

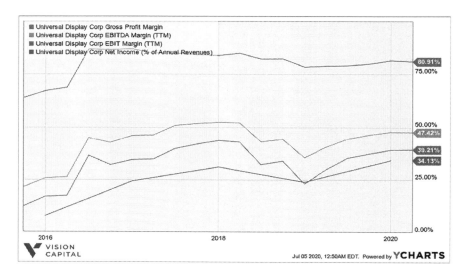

We would prefer to own any of the first three companies **vs the next two** (Sears and General Electric). **Declining profits are usually foretelling that something is not going well** with the company and that they are clearly struggling.

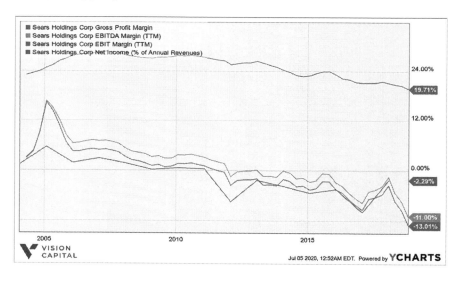

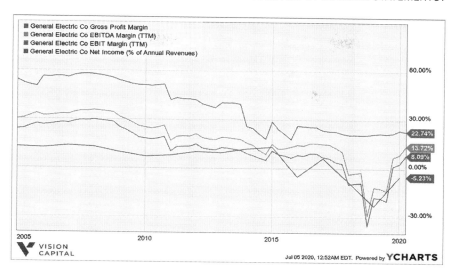

Commitment No. 9

We love companies with growing revenues and profits.

Commitment No. 10

We love companies that especially have operating leverage.

Balance Sheet

We prefer financially strong companies. We prefer them to have **little to no debt, and preferably net cash**.

Net Cash = Add Asset (Cash + Short-Term Investments)
Subtract Liabilities (Short-Term and Long-Term Debt)

Why Net Cash?

Because when there is a financial downturn leading to reduced demand for the company's products and/or services, the company **might find it difficult to refinance their maturing debt** (if they have any). Or when **interest rates are rising**, it can result in **higher interest expenses**, thus **reducing profits and cash flows**. We are looking for companies that can survive such external black-swan events which are **often out of their control** so that they can **survive to thrive**.

Why invest in companies that are subject to such higher risks where there is a higher probability of such a negative scenario that can lead to share price declines? By selectively **avoiding investing in such companies that are typically highly leveraged**, we are **reducing the probability of having significantly underperforming companies** that we own when they run into financial difficulties. The way we think about it is that we do not want to own companies that when in good times, provide maybe average to slightly above returns, but when in bad times can get really bad.

Leverage is not necessarily a bad thing. Some leverage and debt can be good if used in the right manner. For example, if debt is a cheaper way for a company to raise a portion of the capital to fund their business expansion, and if they can do it while not giving up too much equity, this can be positive for the company's debt structure.

Last thoughts, **everything should always be looked at in perspective**. There is no absolute exact amount of net cash one company should have.

Especially for yet to be profitable companies (but improving), we should always **compare relatively** how much **net cash** the company has, **versus** their approximate **existing and expected annual** (1) **net income** and (2) **free cash flow burn**. Typically, if the ratios tend to be at least 3-5 years, we should be more comfortable.

Free cash flow (FCF) and operating cash flow typically should be in the same direction but it keeps differing significantly, one should investigate further to find out why.

Let's look at the examples of four companies below.

1. **Facebook, Inc. (NASDAQ: FB)** is **extremely profitable**, has strong cash flows, and has a strong balance (little debt US$900mil vs OCF US$36.3bn), which if they want, they can easily redeem all their debt anytime.

2. **Shopify Inc (NYSE: SHOP)** is **yet to be profitable** (Net Income of -US$125mil), has zero debt and cash of US$2.45bn, and thus can still stay unprofitable for another 20 years at current unprofitability (but not that we like).

3. **Delta Air Lines Inc (NYSE: DAL) is profitable,** but typically of most airlines, it tends to be an extremely capital-intensive business that requires lots of long-term debt to fund its short-term operations which can be profitable. DAL has US$11.2bn of debt and US$8.3bn of net debt, net income of US$4.8bn is strong but if DAL is subject to an economic downturn or disaster and if their airplanes are unable to fly for more than a couple of months, and if there is insufficient cash to operate the business and pay the interest expenses, they can run into financial difficulties.

4. **Occidental Petroleum Corporation (NYSE: OXY)** is a U.S. oil exploration and production company. OXY is not profitable and their balance sheet has massive amounts of debt (US$38.2bn) vs cash (US$3bn). Should there be an economic downturn and any downturn in oil prices, the company will likely struggle as revenues take a hit both from the demand and the pricing side and might run into financial difficulties.

US$mil	Facebook, Inc.	Shopify Inc	Delta Air Lines Inc	Occidental Petroleum
Cash & ST Investments	+54,900	+2,450	2,882	3,032
ST & LT Debt	+900	0	**11,160**	**38,240**
Net Cash	+54,000	2,450	**-8,278**	**-35,208**
Net Income (TTM)	+18,480	-125	+4,766	**-667**
OCF	+36,310	+70	+8,425	+7375
FCF (Quarterly)	+4,980	+39	**-115**	**-284**

Source: YCharts, data as of 18 March 2020

Commitment No. 11

We love companies that are financially strong and preferably have net cash.

Hopefully, with these four examples, we are starting to give you a flavor for the companies that we prefer and why. Ultimately, we **don't want to invest** in companies that are **good during good times, but when bad times occur, it can be really bad.** That's **not how we prefer to invest.** We wouldn't like to roll a dice and receive average returns 5 out of 6 times and a very bad loss 1 out of 6 times. This works against us when we invest for the long-term.

We prefer to **invest** in companies that will **do amazingly well when times are good, and still okay when times are bad.** We prefer the odds to be in our favor. That is just our preference. We prefer to roll a dice that gives us above-average returns maybe 4-5 times out of 6, and 1-2 times out of 6 gives us average / below-average returns. Because when we invest for the long term, we will still get overall above-average returns when we invest like that.

YTD 2020 Returns vs S&P 500: DAL and OXY Fell Much More Than S&P 500

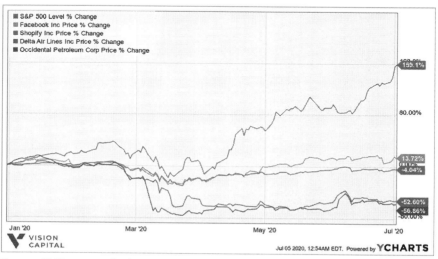

Source: YCharts as of July 5, 2020.

Drag from Having Too Much Cash

Having too much cash likewise sitting in a company's balance sheet and **invested in low yielding investments** (government bonds, municipal and agency bonds, etc.) is not good either. It can present a potential drag on the company as the company is **sitting on too much unused cash and not putting it to good use**. There is a balance as to how much cash a company should have, and this varies from industry and at what phase the company is in as they grow. If a company is making too much profits and is unable to invest the cash quick enough and to meet sufficient return hurdle rates, they should be returning the capital back to shareholders via dividends or share buybacks.

Cash Flow Statement

If earnings is queen, **cash flow is king**. Why? Because if a company is profitable but does not have sufficient cash in the interim to run its business, it can run into financial difficulties and might have to liquidate its business or worse case, file for bankruptcy.

> *"Markets can remain irrational for longer*
> *than you can remain solvent"*
> *- John Maynard Keynes).*

What Is a Cash Flow Statement?

The statement of cash flows, or cash flow statement, is a financial statement that summarizes the amount of **cash and cash equivalents entering and leaving a company**.

The cash flow statement reveals a company's financial health and **measures how well a company manages its cash position**, meaning how well the company generates cash to pay its debt obligations and fund its operating expenses.

The three main components of the cash flow statement are:

1. **Cash from Operating Activities**
2. **Cash from Investing Activities**
3. **Cash from Financing Activities**

It's important to note that the **cash flow statement is distinct** from the income statement and balance sheet because it **does not include the amount of future incoming and outgoing cash that has been recorded on credit**. Therefore, cash is not the same as net income, which can contain non-cash items.

We focus on two main components of what we look out for in the cash flow statement:

1. **Operating Cash Flow (OCF)** and **Free Cash Flow (FCF)**
2. **Cash Conversion Cycle** (CCC)

Simplified Formulas

Operating Cash Flow (OCF) = Net Income + Non-cash Expenses (e.g. depreciation, amortization & stock-based comp) – Increase in non-cash Net Working Capital (e.g. receivables, payables & inventory)

Free Cash Flow (FCF) = OCF - Capital Expenditures (Capex)

Operating Cash Flow and Free Cash Flow

Growth in OCF and FCF drives Long Term increase in Share Price

The following two charts for Apple and Amazon should be very clear to illustrate the point that **positive and growing cash flows ultimately drive the business's growth** and **eventually its share price**.

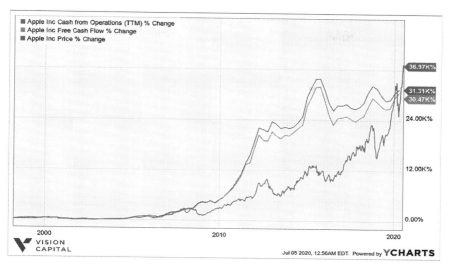

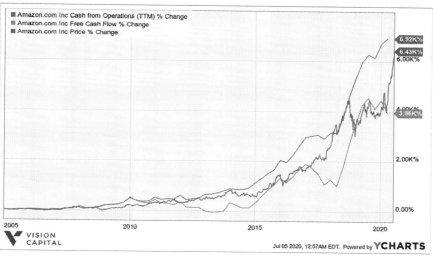

Decline in OCF and FCF Will Move the Share Price Slower

Conversely, the following two charts for Sears and General Electric should be very clear to illustrate the point that **cash flows ultimately drive the business's growth** and **eventually its share price**. If a company is not growing its top-line / revenues and not making money and is struggling to generate positive cash flows, the market will know and the share price will follow eventually and decline. From this, you should come to realize that the decline of companies does not happen in a single month or day; they usually take time over months if not years, and the market and the investors will eventually reflect accordingly.

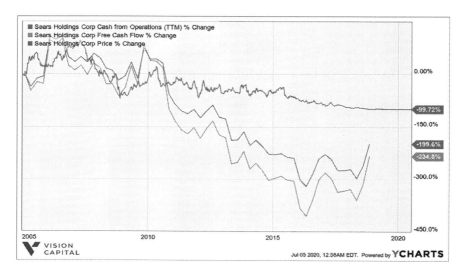

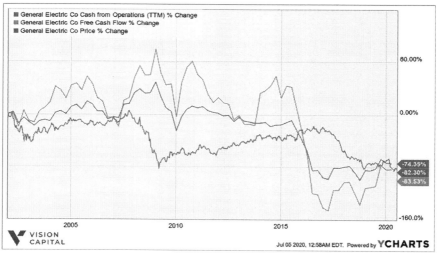

Commitment No. 12

We love companies with growing revenues, profits, and cash flows.

Cash Conversion Cycle

Cash Conversion Cycle (CCCS)	$CCC = DIO + DSO - DPO$	The lower (or even more negative), the better
Days Inventory Outstanding (DIO)	$\dfrac{\text{Average Inventory}}{\text{Cost of Goods Sold (COGS)}}$	The **lower**, the better
Days Sales Outstanding (DSO)	$\dfrac{\text{Average Accounts Receivables}}{\text{Revenue}}$	The **lower**, the better
Days Payables Outstanding (DPO)	$\dfrac{\text{Average Accounts Payables}}{\text{Cost of Goods Sold (COGS)}}$	The **higher**, the better

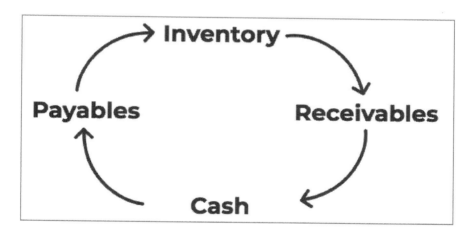

1. **Days Inventory Outstanding (DIO)** is the number of days, on average, it takes a company **to turn its inventory into sales**. Essentially, DIO is the average number of days that a company holds its inventory before selling it.
2. **Days Sales Outstanding (DSO)** is the number of days, on average, it **takes a company to collect its receivables**. Therefore,

DSO measures the average number of days for a company to collect payment after a sale.

3. **Days Payable Outstanding (DPO)** is the number of days, on average, it takes a **company to pay back its payables**. Therefore, DPO measures the average number of days for a company to pay its invoices from trade creditors, i.e., suppliers.

4. **Cash Conversion Cycle (CCC)** is aimed at **assessing how efficiently a company is managing its working capital**. As with other cash flow calculations, the **shorter the cash conversion cycle**, the better the company is at selling inventories and recovering cash from these sales while taking longer to pay suppliers.

Let me use two examples of **Costco Wholesale Corporation (NASDAQ: COST)** and **Apple Inc. (NASDAQ: AAPL)** to illustrate:

(1) Costco Wholesale Corporation

Below is a partial business description from Costco's 10K Annual Report:

*Costco operates membership warehouses based on the concept that offering our members low prices on a limited selection of nationally branded and private-label products in a wide range of categories will **produce high sales volumes and rapid inventory turnover**. When combined with the operating efficiencies achieved by volume purchasing, efficient distribution and reduced handling of merchandise in no-frills, self-service warehouse facilities, these volumes and turnover enable us to operate profitably at significantly lower gross margins (net sales less merchandise costs) than most other retailers. We **generally sell inventory before we are required to pay for it**, even while taking advantage of early payment discounts[33].*

As you can see below, Costco's takes on **average 3.829 days to sell their products (DSP)**, their average **inventory sits on the shelf for 30.81 days** before the products are sold (DIO) and Costco takes on average **31.39**

---

[33] Source: Costco's Wholesale's 2019 10-K Annual Report https://investor.costco.com/static-files/05c62fe6-6c09-4e16-8d8b-5e456e5a0f7e

days to pay their suppliers. As a result, Costco uses cash for 3.252 days for every $1 of product sold in the entire process.

Costco's CCC vs DSO, DIO & DPO

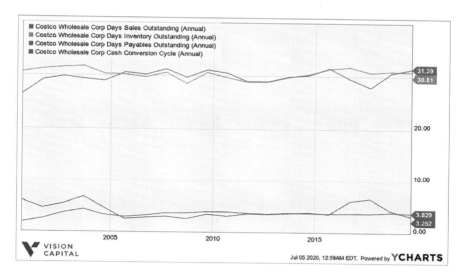

Costco Has One of the Lowest Cash Conversion Cycle Amongst Its Competitors

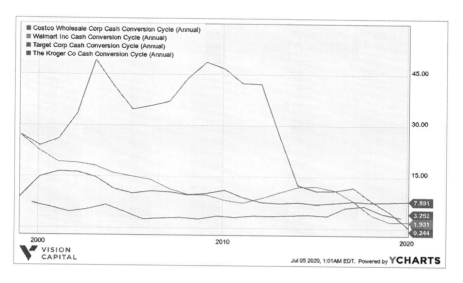

(2) Apple Inc

Below is an excerpt from Apple's 2019 10K annual report[34]:

*"The Company **sells its products** and resells third-party products in most of its major markets **directly** to consumers, small and mid-sized businesses, and education, enterprise and government customers **through its retail and on-line stores and its direct sales force**. The Company also employs a **variety of indirect distribution channels**, such as third-party cellular network carriers, wholesalers, retailers, and resellers.*

*"**Substantially all of the Company's manufacturing is performed in whole or in part by outsourcing partners ...to supply and manufacture many components,** and on outsourcing partners primarily located in Asia**, for final assembly of substantially all of the Company's hardware product.**"*

After reading this, the following chart should become extremely apparent. Apple takes 115 days on average to pay its suppliers (DPO), 66 days on average to receive from its customers (DSO), and 9 days on average for a product to fly off its shelves (DIO). **Apple has a negative Cash Conversion Cycle (CCC) of almost 40 days.** This means **Apple gets free 40 days of free financing from their suppliers to do business**. Apple does not need any cash to sell their product. Would you like to own such a business? We definitely would like to! And you might grow to start liking and seeing the word "**Outsourcing!**"

---

[34] Source: Apple Inc's 2019 10K Annual Report
https://d18rn0p25nwr6d.cloudfront.net/CIK-0000320193/1a919118-a594-44f3-92f0-4ecca47b1a7d.pdf#page4

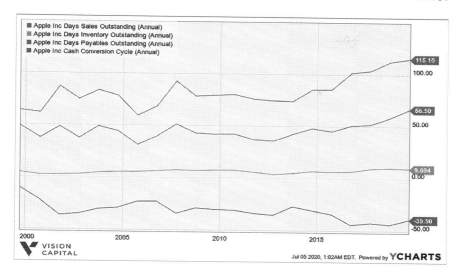

Commitment No. 13

We especially love companies with negative CCC that get paid to do business.

"**Cash ... is to a business as oxygen is to an individual**:
never thought about when it is present, the only
thing **in mind when it is absent**"
- Warren Buffett

We especially love companies with negative cash conversion cycles. Truthfully, we believe there are probably only a handful of companies in the world that are like that. But **having a negative cash conversion cycle is not an absolute must**. It really depends on the industry the company is in, the business model of the company itself. But we **definitely prefer companies that have lower cash conversion cycles**.

QUICK SUMMARY

- Earnings drive the **long-term share price** of a company.
- Invest in **profitable companies** or companies that **may not currently be profitable but have improving profit margins**.
- Analyze a company's profitability by looking for **increasing revenues and even faster growing profits** by seeing if expenses can increase at a decreasing rate, and profits increasing at an even faster rate.

CHAPTER 10

WHY DO WE AVOID TURNAROUNDS, CYCLICALS, ASSET PLAYS, SLOW GROWERS, AND STALWARTS BUT LIKE FAST GROWERS?

Peter Lynch classifies all stocks **into roughly six categories**:

1. Slow Growers
2. Stalwarts (Mid-Growers)
3. Fast Growers
4. Cyclicals
5. Asset Plays
6. Turnaround

Let's go through these six categories in greater detail:

(1) Slow Growers

Slow growers are just what the name implies, these are **typically large, mature companies that are generally older** with **earnings growth lower**

than the country's GDP growth. Slow growth isn't necessarily a stigma, as many companies in this category are **remarkably consistent and provide regular dividends for investors**. The payment of cash dividends is the main return of slow growth stocks for shareholders.

(2) Stalwarts

Stalwarts are companies **with high single-digit to low double-digit growth**. They are medium-growth stocks that typically range from **medium to large-sized companies**. Stalwarts are generally **resilient to recessions or economic downturns**. They are mostly multibillion-dollar giants that are slow to push out new products but remain strong with recession-proof products.

(3) Fast Growers

Fast growers refer to **high growth stocks** of companies with **double-digit earnings growth rates**. These are mainly small and expanding companies that are gaining market share faster than other companies in the industry. Fast growers are much favored by Lynch, as these stocks can **potentially turn into 10 baggers**, an investment that appreciates to 10 times its initial purchase price. However, it is also worth noting that these stocks **also come with higher risk**.

(4) Cyclicals

A cyclical company is one "**whose sales and profits rise and fall regularly in a completely predictable fashion**." The expansion and contraction of sales is typical of these companies. Cyclical companies typically fall under industries such as **airline, automotive, chemical**, etc.

(5) Turnarounds

Turnarounds are **companies whose share prices have plummeted due to force majeure, accidents, or unfortunate events**. For example, in the 1980s, Chrysler was the star turnaround stock. It was on the verge of bankruptcy and in desperate need of a US$1.5 billion loan from the federal government. Clearly, turnarounds **have tremendous potential for great gains**, but you need to consider the risks very carefully. Timing is essential in buying these stocks, as their operations recover and normalize.

(6) Asset Plays

Asset plays are **stocks with valuable assets**. This could include cash, properties, investments, or trademarks. Their share price is **trading below the value of their assets (NAV = Net Asset Value)**. Given this trait, **patience** is the most important aspect when investing in these companies, for **it may be a while** before you actually see any profit from it.

Why Not Turnarounds, Cyclicals, Asset Plays, Slow Growers, and Stalwarts but Fast Growers Instead?

Why Not?

1. **Slow Growers:** Yes slow growers are steady, but if they are **growing slower and at less** than GDP, that means they are likely (1) the **leader with a large market share** and/or (2) in a **market limited in upside growth**. That means these companies are **likely to return slightly above to below-average returns over the long term**. Because of the law of large numbers, the bigger a company gets, the harder it must work to outperform the market. It is harder to steer an aircraft carrier than a tugboat. Yes, they could potentially provide higher returns than bank deposit rates or bonds, but the **upside is likely extremely limited**, and **should a few of these companies eventually start declining**, they will lose more than those single-digit returns. That can **tilt your portfolio to underperformance**.

    "From Dow Chemical to Tampa Electric, the highfliers
    of one decade become the groundhogs of the next."
    - Peter Lynch

2. **Stalwarts (Mid-Growers):** Investors in such companies **could typically expect average to slightly above average returns over the long term,** driven by faster than expected sales and earnings growth. But we will watch if our stalwarts start becoming slow growers and growth starts declining with time. Not that we dislike stalwarts, just that holding these, one **might not expect significant market-beating returns over time.**

3. **Cyclicals:** Cyclicals **can provide strong outperformance if you can perfectly time** the absolute bottom to enter and buy these stocks and sell them right at the top. **If you have the foresight of perfect timing** and can do so, by all means, you should go ahead. But if you are **unable to do so**, like most investors, including the best ones out there, it might be **better to avoid that**. Recall what we discussed earlier: **perfectly timing only gives us a bit more in returns over the long run versus a buy and hold,** but **if we miss the best days**, it can **significantly impact our returns much more negatively.** For those reasons, we tend to avoid cyclical companies.

"Stop trying to predict…" – *Warren Buffett*

"Market timing is impossible to perfect." - *Mark Riepe*

"Only liars manage to always be out during bad times and in during good times."
- Bernard Baruch

4. **Asset Plays:** When investing in undervalued asset plays, the **downside tends to be much less** versus other types because of the **entry (to buy) is typically significantly below NAV.** Though this is not to say that it cannot go lower, but it **can potentially take a long time** for the value to be realized back to NAV or higher. Because the upside is potentially limited to NAV or a slight premium to it, one often does not get massive multibagger opportunities with respect to asset plays. In addition, there is **already fierce**

competition in asset plays, which are typically well tracked by the fund managers who are better equipped to trade around these. To us, buying something and selling something in the short to medium term, we are not utilizing the odds of long term investing in our favor. That is not to say that it does not work, but it is much more difficult to do so and thus, we do not want to set exemptions.

5. **Turnarounds:**

We avoid investing in turnaround businesses. Turnarounds are **businesses that are experiencing temporary challenges** such as business transitions, product issues, management change, or temporary shifts in customers' preferences, resulting in a huge decline in demand for the business's products and services, declining revenues, profits, and cash flows. **We do not prefer to invest in turnarounds** because there is usually a bigger reason for the downward decline and going against such inertia is extremely difficult.

It is **not to say that it is impossible for companies to turnaround**; it's just that the **odds are stacked against turnarounds**. Yes, that can be great rewards if you invest in a turnaround and it does; you can be richly rewarded. With turnarounds, the odds of failing and going to zero (if bankruptcy or liquidation) are 4-5 times out of 6, and the odds of it succeeding are 1-2 times out of 6 where you can perhaps get 1-3 times of your capital. The only way to play this is via a short to medium term tactical entry (buy) and exit (sell).

Since we are only long-term buy and hold investors, unless a turnaround changes their business model significantly such that it warrants a further look, we will not bother. The analogy would be, I'd rather spend more to buy a tree that is healthy and strong than to buy a tree that is dying on the cheap anytime. Why go against inertia **when there are so many other better businesses to invest and own**?

> *"It's smarter to invest in large but fantastic companies*
> ***than to buy a mediocre business just because it's cheap."***
> *- Warren Buffett*

The following are two charts of two companies, **Sears and Crocs**. It tells two tales. For Sears, the inevitable shift away from brick & mortar retail and the failure to revamp eventually led to the collapse. For Crocs, it really is still the issue with the product: its brightly colored clogs. You can try to turnaround, but if there's a fundamental problem with your product and it's the end of the fad, that imposes limitations, even if we hire the best CEO in the world. Do you want to swim against the tide? **We rather swim with the tide anytime, not against it**. That's why we **almost never invest in turnarounds**.

> *"After 25 years of buying and supervising a great variety of businesses,*
> *Charlie and I **have not learned how to solve***
> ***difficult business problems**.*
> ***What we have learned is to avoid them**."*
> *- Warren Buffett*

> *"**Wonderful** businesses are likely to **remain wonderful for decades**.*
> ***Bad** businesses **remain bad for a long time**."*
> *- Warren Buffett*

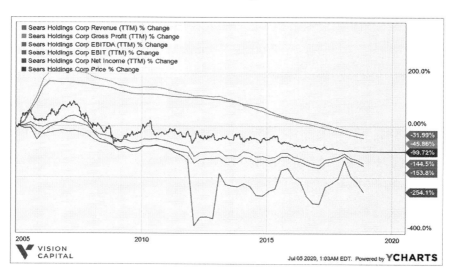

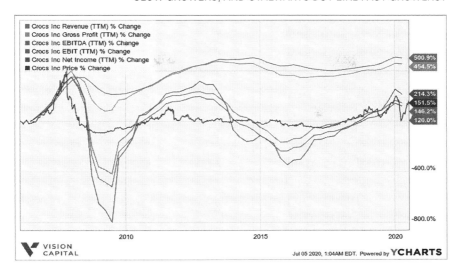

Then Why Fast Growers?

6. **Fast Growers**: We like Fast Growers because of **massive multi-bagger opportunities**. When we employ a thorough framework, it allows us to sieve out the needles from the haystack easily; we are **not randomly throwing darts**. We are **looking for the best, the most innovative, the financially strongest businesses that are founder-owned and led with massive tailwinds and a growing market**. And when we find these companies and own them for the long-term, **these multibagger winners tend to contribute returns that can even gain more than 10X / 1000%** over the long run. And the **overwhelming gains from your winners will tend to contribute to the majority of your portfolio gains and outweigh the losses from your losers over time. Your losers will become more and more insignificant over time**. That's how we prefer to invest, and we hope you do too.

*"I **find excellence, buy excellence**, and **add to excellence** over time.*
*I **sell mediocrity**. That's **how I invest**."*
- David Gardner

135

*"**Buy the best** stocks, **sell the losing** stocks, and **avoid the worst** stocks."*
- Howard Marks

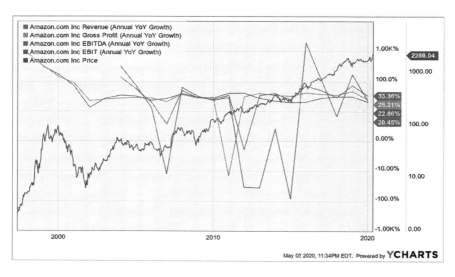

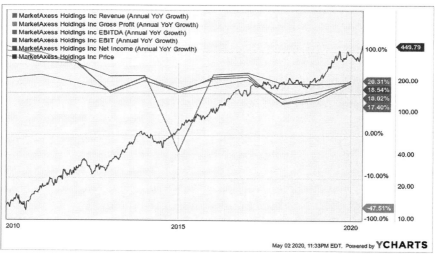

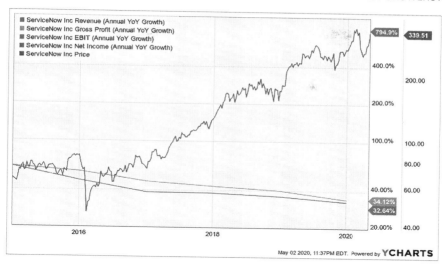

Commitment No. 14

We commit to finding excellence, buying excellence, and adding to excellence over time. We sell mediocrity. That's how we invest.

Commitment No. 15

We almost never invest in turnaround companies.

QUICK SUMMARY

- Invest in **fast growers** for massive multibagger opportunities.
- Look for **the best, the most innovative, the financially strongest businesses** that are founder-owned and led with massive tailwinds and a growing market.
- We **avoid investing** in stalwarts, cyclicals, slow growers, asset plays, and turnarounds.

CHAPTER 11

WHY IS UNDERSTANDING YOUR OWN CIRCLE OF COMPETENCE IMPORTANT?

Understanding your circle of competence helps you avoid problems, identify opportunities for improvement, and learn from others.

The concept of the **Circle of Competence** has been used over the years by Warren Buffett as a way to focus investors on only operating in areas they knew best. The bones of the concept appear in his 1996 Shareholder Letter[35]:

"What an investor needs is the ability to correctly evaluate selected businesses. Note that word "selected": **You don't have to be an expert on every company or even many. You only have to be able to evaluate companies within your circle of competence.** *The* **size of that circle** *is* **not very important; knowing its boundaries, however, is vital.**"

---

[35] Source: Berkshire Hathaway 1996 Shareholder Letter
https://www.berkshirehathaway.com/letters/1996.html

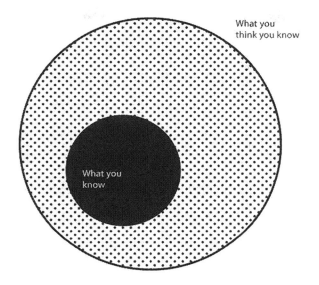

The simple takeaway here is clear. **If you want to improve your odds of success in life and business**, then **define the perimeter of your circle of competence** and **operate inside of it. Over time, work to expand that circle** but never fool yourself about where it stands today, and never be afraid to say, "I don't know."

What Other Companies Do We Tend to Avoid Investing In?

1. We tend to **avoid companies in cyclical industries** such as **oil and gas, property development and construction, semiconductor, shipping/ship-building, commodity trading companies, automotive, and banks**.
2. We tend to **avoid companies that deal with vice products and services like alcohol, tobacco, military-industrial equipment, illicit drugs, and gambling** because that is the world and business we prefer to own.
3. We tend to **avoid pure brick and mortar businesses** because **growth is not infinitely scalable** and has to be followed with physical store openings. Exceptions can be considered.

4. We tend to **avoid pharmaceutical companies**. I am not a doctor, I don't have strong medical knowledge, and because of the nature of pharmaceutical companies (for example in the U.S., the FDA process can be highly unpredictable), we avoid pharmaceuticals. I don't like investing in lottery-type payoffs where if it is successful, we will get massive 10X, 50X gains but if it fails, the stock will lose 50-90% of its value.

5. We **do not invest in turnarounds, cigar butts, value plays**.

We bet you must be thinking right now, "Is that every other business that is listed? Are there any other businesses that I can invest in and own?"

What we have provided is learning from our own lessons over the years and from the experiences of others. We would like you to come up with your own list, your own circle of competence (remember it can expand with time). Ultimately, **it has to be a business that you want to own for the long term**. If you find a business that you can see yourself owning for the next ten years and you know that it will still do well, by all means, go ahead!

We **want you to create your own circle of competence** and what businesses you have extreme expertise in and are actually comfortable with. And always remember your circle of competence is **never static**; it is constantly evolving, and it **can definitely expand as you learn** more about other new businesses and industries.

As Warren Buffett rightly shares countless pieces of wisdom:

1. **Keep it Simple. Never invest in a company whose business you don't understand.** Risk comes from not knowing what you're doing.

2. **Don't invest** in a company **just because someone told you to**. **Always do your own due diligence** (DYODD). **Take full responsibility** for your own investments and your own decisions, never blame someone else or find an excuse to justify.

3. **Understand what your core competence** is. As a general rule, **if I can't clearly explain what a company does, how it makes**

money, and how it could grow in a few sentences, I won't invest in it.

4. **Buy into a company because you want to own it**, not because you want the stock to go up.

5. **Do not think of your investments as "stocks,"** but **think of buying a stock as buying an entire business**.

6. **Buy a stock the way you would buy a house.** Understand and like it such that you'd be content to own it in the absence of any market.

7. If you **aren't willing to own a stock for ten years**, don't even think about owning it for ten minutes.

8. Charlie and I view the marketable common stocks that Berkshire **owns as interests in businesses, not as ticker symbols to be bought or sold based on their "chart" patterns, the "target" prices of analysts, or the opinions of media pundits.**

QUICK SUMMARY

- Understanding your **circle of competence** makes you a more accomplished investor.
- Invest only in businesses **you understand**.
- **Buy into a company you want to own, into a business**, not because you have hopes on the stock price increasing.

CHAPTER 12

WHY DO WE LOVE FOUNDER-OWNED AND LED COMPANIES?

Founder-Led Companies Tend to Outperform Manager Led Companies on Average:

1. **Share price** (3.1x times 1990-2014, Bain)
2. **Revenue growth, R&D, and Capex expenditure**
3. **Generated 30% more patents**

- 7% of 3,600 globally listed companies with **market capitalizations above $500 million are run by their founders.**
- **Among IPOs, the tendency is more common; 30%** of the companies listed globally over the last five years are **led by their founders**.
- **Majority of founder-led companies are listed in the U.S. (70%),** followed by China (8%), Japan (7%) and Europe (6%), and the majority operate in the technology, pharmaceuticals, and retail sectors. Their **tendency to be technology businesses,** and America's history of innovation, seem the most obvious reason for this distribution. In addition, they tend to be largely an **American West-Coast phenomenon.**

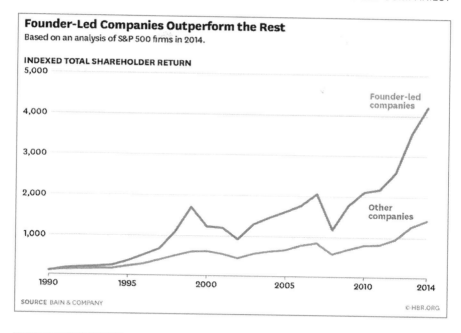

Founder-Led Companies Outperform the Rest
Based on an analysis of S&P 500 firms in 2014.

INDEXED TOTAL SHAREHOLDER RETURN

SOURCE BAIN & COMPANY

©HBR.ORG

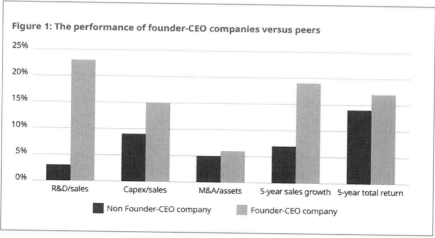

Figure 1: The performance of founder-CEO companies versus peers

■ Non Founder-CEO company   ■ Founder-CEO company

Source: Harvard Business Review[36] (1990-2014)

[36] Source: Harvard Business Review
https://hbr.org/2016/03/founder-led-companies-outperform-the-rest-heres-why

Selected Founder-led and Owned S&P 500 Companies That Have Outperformed Over the Last 10 years

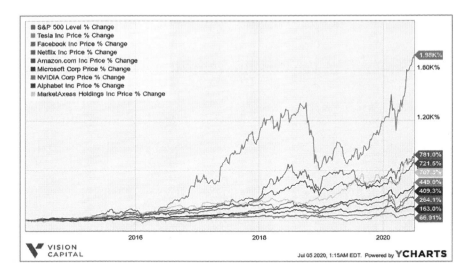

Why Do Founder CEOs Outperform?

A number of theories have attempted to explain founder-led company outperformance. From our perspective, we think the following 11 aspects make the most sense:

1. The Founder's Mentality

There are three key elements that tend to distinguish founder-led firms with respect to their mentality:

1. **An extraordinary sense of insurgency.** Founders are very clear about the "big why" of their companies' purpose—and the company is at war with the industry on behalf of underserved customers.
2. **A frontline obsession.** Zook says founders are so committed to developing customer loyalty and advocacy that they empower frontline employees with the authority to solve problems and invent better solutions and products.

3. **An owner's mindset**, which includes an aversion to bureaucracy, a bias for action, and a strong cash focus.

2. Better-Aligned Management Incentives

We believe **founder CEOs almost always own a large amount of equity** in the business. Typically, the net worth of a founder is closely bound up with the companies they create. With their own wealth at risk, the **incentives are aligned** with shareholders, as the **CEOs have extra motivation to make the business succeed**.

Because of the large ownership stakes, we believe founders **tend to think of what is best for a business long-term** (we like long term not short term anyway). Professional CEOs tend to own far less stock than founders do. They can be fired at any moment, and their average tenure is only eight years. As a result, they tend to be very short-term focused by nature and have more reason to focus on next year's bonus than the company's performance 20 years from now. By contrast, a founder CEO with a large equity stake typically has **greater incentive to plan for the long term**, as well as more job security to ensure they stay around to enjoy it. That's why founder-led companies **spend more money investing in the future through R&D and patents** than companies run by professional or "agent" CEOs.

3. Top-Down Culture

In our opinion, **starting and growing a company from nothing** to a $10- or $20 million-dollar business **is a feat in and of itself**. We believe founders are accustomed to wearing multiple hats, are likely good at a variety of tasks, and generally go the extra mile for customers based on these roots. This culture naturally imbues down and has been termed the "founders touch." This effect can promote a culture of flexibility, long-term thinking, innovation, commitment to customers, and employee loyalty.

4. Irreplaceable Knowledge and Moral Authority

No one knows a company better than its founder. Founders are the ones who identified the original market opportunity, innovated a new solution, discovered competitors' strengths and weaknesses; have personal knowledge of every employee hired, every product made, every customer won. This **"pyramid of knowledge" is impossible to replicate** and serves as the foundation for new innovations going forward. Founders also have the moral authority to make major changes when necessary. They know the business better than anyone else does. Moreover, since they originally made the decisions that shaped the company, stakeholders trust them to overturn those decisions when the time comes.

5. Purpose and Long-Term Commitment

In our opinion, there are **profound differences in the perspectives** of professional CEOs and founder CEOs. We think professional CEOs tend to be primarily motivated by job-related rewards, such as compensation, reputation, career advancement, and job security, which can be measured and doled out on fairly short-term time scales. By contrast, **for many founder CEOs, their company may be their life's work**, with their emotional commitment exceeding their equity stake many times over. We believe they **often seek to build something of significance and purpose**, and they **naturally take a long-term view** of their companies. It is our opinion that these different perspectives drive significant differences in the way these two types of leaders run their companies.

6. Pride

Pride can affect executive behavior, leading to a difference in performance that in turn leads to **more motivated, more loyal, and harder-working employees**. A founder walks into his company's headquarters, and it may be his name that is above the door. Not only is that motivating for the founder, but it may be motivating for employees as well. Employees may be very happy to be working for a visionary in their industry, and that makes them work a little harder.

7. Social Capital

Company founders build up a storehouse of social capital by creating a company and providing jobs and a **sense of purpose for their employees**. As a result, they may have an easier time inspiring and leading the organization, which leads to better products, happier customers, and smarter decision making throughout the company.

8. Frugality

We believe there is a fundamental psychological difference in the way agent CEOs and founder CEOs look at spending. To a professional manager, a budget is a budget; **to a founder, a budget feels like personal money**. Founders learn frugality during the early days of the business and retain that attitude even after their companies become large businesses. The result can be closer attention to the bottom line, greater reinvestment in the long-term, and less temptation to fritter away cash on flashy acquisitions.

9. Healthy Paranoia

Founders **tend to have a healthy paranoia** about their business. They understand their company's strengths, but because they are so **protective of their creation**, they rarely downplay the risks of being disrupted. This **paranoia drives them to stay on top** of emerging industry trends and constantly rebuild their competitive defenses, so their business can remain sustainable in the long run.

10. Smarter Capital Allocation Decisions

Management's job is to run the day-to-day business and make careful decisions on capital allocations. With profits, there are five ways they can allocate it. They can re-invest in the business, acquire another company, pay down debt, pay out a dividend, or buy back their own stock. In our opinion, hired management has more of an incentive to boost short-term profits to receive bonuses, even if it may be problematic or downright disastrous in the long run. We believe **founders tend to take a longer-term view when it comes to capital allocation**, as they spent so much time building the business, do not want to ruin it for short-term reasons, and want a prosperous future.

11. Innovation

Founder CEOs **innovate from day one when they start their businesses**, and we think the evidence suggests that their instinct to innovate persists. Founder CEOs **tend to invest more in R&D** than non-founder CEOs, which inherently leads to increased spending in the short term, but greater sustainability in the long term.

Remember Not All Founders Are Created Equal

Although it is clear **founders as a whole tend to outperform the broad market, one can do better picking the best of the founder-led companies**, versus passively investing in the group as a whole.

As Warren Buffett famously said, "When a management with a reputation for brilliance tackles a business with a reputation for bad economics, it is the **reputation of the business that remains intact**."

Thus, we believe it is important to **take into consideration industry margins, competitive products/services**, etc.

Further, we feel it is important to 1) look at the **founder's long-term track record;** 2) look for a **strong business model** with **clear long-term competitive advantages**.

In our opinion, **a wonderful business, run by a founder CEO with a long track record of compounding the business value is a business we want to own.**

Commitment No. 16

We prefer to own businesses that are founder-led and owned that have a good track record of running the business.

Companies Often Take Time to Become Poor and Leave Clues for Us

The good thing for us investors is that **good companies almost never become poor companies overnight**. Typically, it **tends to happen over time**, and they are always throwing hints at us. Losing market share, innovation, and lack of vision, are some typical clues we should be consistently on the lookout for.

For every Sergey Brin, there is a **Michael Dell**. While the Google co-founder and CEO made his company one of the most valuable in the world with its shares trading near an all-time high, **Dell has laid waste to his namesake**. Dell and financial supporters offered to buy the company for $13.65 a share, 40% lower than what it was worth when Dell returned to the company as CEO in early 2007.

Dell's failure is not unique. Michael Dell belongs to a group of founders of large listed public companies that **showed great promise** but were **ultimately wrecked by poor decisions, legal problems, and a lack of innovation**.

A more complex measurement of these founders' performance is their **lack of vision** to transform their companies as the markets in which they operate change. Dell **did not drive any comparable revolution** at his company, which never stepped aggressively into the new age of personal computing— tablets and smartphones.

Dell, founded 1984

Founder: Michael Dell, 13.97% voting share

Dell started his company when he was 19 years old. By 2001, the company he founded as a college student was the largest computer systems provider in the world. In 2004, Dell resigned as CEO but returned to the position in February 2007. By then, the <u>company had already begun to lose its appeal with consumers in the competitive PC business</u>. Despite

Dell's return, the <u>company continued to struggle in its core business. Dell's worldwide PC market share fell from 15.9% in 2006 to 10.7% in 2012</u>. Consumers' growing preferences for tablets and smartphones over PCs and regulatory scrutiny have hurt the company. In 2010, the <u>SEC fined Dell $100 million, and Michael Dell $4 million, alleging the company engaged in accounting fraud intended to mislead investors about financial performance</u>. On Feb. 5, Dell reached a deal with a group of investors that included Michael Dell to go private for $24.4 billion, the largest leveraged buyout since the 2008 financial crisis.[37]

QUICK SUMMARY

- **Founder-led companies** outperform manger led companies.
- Own a wonderful business, **run by a founder CEO** with a long track record of compounding the business.
- Watch out for persistent clues if a **good company is becoming poor.**

---

[37] Source: USA Today "Eight founders who ruined their companies" https://www.us-atoday.com/story/money/business/2013/02/09/founders-ruin-companies/1905921/

C H A P T E R 1 3

WHY DO WE LIKE COMPANIES WITH STRONG COMPETITIVE ADVANTAGES?

What Is an Economic Moat or Competitive Advantage?

The concept of the economic moat **comes from Warren Buffett**. The term refers to a **company's ability to maintain a competitive advantage over its rivals** and **thus protect its long-term profitability and market share and earn outsized profits over time**. Buffett's investment strategy centers on **companies with strong economic moats**, as they are more likely to withstand their competitors and remain successful. Thus, the **strength and sustainability of the moat are extremely key**.

> *"The **key to successful investing** is to **determine if a company has durable competitive advantage. Companies with durable competitive advantage consistently deliver outstanding results for investors**,"*
> *- Warren Buffett*

Why Companies Need a Competitive Advantage

A **competitive advantage** is any quality that enables a company to offer similar products to its peers while **enjoying superior financial**

performance. Over time, companies are more likely to lose their competitive advantage because as they grow increasingly profitable, competitors are more likely to replicate their methods or create even better ones.

Establishing economic moats can help companies protect their long-term profits. There are several ways in which a company can create an economic moat, and it's possible for a company to have more than one.

*"A good business is like a strong castle with a **deep, wide, and long-lasting moat** around it. I want sharks in the moat. I want it untouchable. The **moat can protect a terrific economic castle with an honest lord in charge of the castle**."*
- Warren Buffett

Four Questions to Think About

1. What is the **goal** of the business?
2. How does the business **make money**?
3. How well is the business **actually doing**?
4. How well is the business **positioned relative to its competitors**?

If you can answer these four questions, you should be able to get a good handle on a business's goals and on its performance just by reading about it and studying its financial statements. It's really the last question, the one in which we consider how well a company is positioned relative to its competitors, where we might need some more help.

Let's try to put together a framework that can separate really great companies from the merely good ones. After all, it is the great companies that will truly keep on doing well and that's what we are trying to find. **We want to find excellence, not mediocrity**.

Four Steps to Determine Whether a Company Has an Economic Moat

1. Evaluate the firm's historical profitability.

Has the firm been able to generate a solid return on its assets and on shareholder equity (i.e. ROA & ROE)? This is probably the most important component in identifying whether or not a company has a moat. While much about assessing a moat is qualitative, the bedrock of analyzing a company still relies on solid financial metrics.

We want to look for companies that are either:

1. **Already profitable with positive stable/increasing returns**
2. **Yet to be profitable and has negative, but improving returns**

2. Assuming that the firm has solid returns on its capital and is consistently profitable, try to identify the source of those profits.

Is the **source** an advantage that only this company has, or is it one that other companies **can easily imitate**? The harder it is for a rival to imitate an advantage, the more likely the company has a barrier to entry in its industry and a source of economic profit.

3. Estimate how long the company will be able to keep competitors at bay.

We refer to this **time period** as the company's competitive advantage period, and it **can be as short as several months or as long as several decades**. The **longer** the competitive advantage period, the **wider** the economic moat. For example, technology or pharmaceutical companies have patents that have a specific life that prevents other competitors from trying to replicate their product or service.

4. Think about the industry's competitive structure.

What is the market share of the company in the industry? Is it a monopoly where largely one company dominates, two companies dominate in a duopoly, or is it an oligopoly where there are many players? Or is it extremely competitive with little way to differentiate? Does it have many profitable firms or is it hypercompetitive with only a few companies scrounging for the last dollar? Highly competitive industries will likely offer less attractive profit growth over the long haul.

We want to look for companies that are either:

1. **Top Dog** in their **existing industry** with either the 1st or 2nd **largest market share** and **still growing their share** in an ever-**growing emerging and important market.**
2. **First Mover** in a **new and rapidly growing, emerging, and important market** gaining market share rapidly with few or little competitors.

Five Different Types of Competitive Advantages

(1) Cost Advantage

Companies that can **deliver or produce better goods or services at a lower cost** than their competition have a major advantage over the competition because they can undercut their competitors on price. Allowing them to either have a **fatter profit margin** or the **same profit margin** as the competitors, but in theory **higher volume** and higher asset turnover. Companies with long-term sustainable cost advantages can command and maintain a large market share within their respective industries, thus forcing competitors out. Wal-Mart and Costco are a good example of a company that maintains a cost advantage, in part by buying and selling huge volumes of goods. Meanwhile, Apple leverages its brand power to squeeze lower prices out of its suppliers, which are eager to deal with this titan of consumer tech.

(2) The Network Effect

The network effect occurs when the **value of a good or service grows as more people use it**. A good example of the network effect is Amazon, whose ever-growing user base offers continuous value to buyers and sellers.

(3) High Switching Costs

Switching costs are expenses or disruptions a customer will encounter when switching from one product or service to another. It's beneficial for companies to create high switching costs, as doing so can help them retain customers. Mobile phone service providers, for example, can lock in customers because of their high switching costs. To change providers, a customer might need to terminate an existing contract and purchase a new phone, both of which can be costly. As such, customers might be less motivated to switch providers even if they are dissatisfied with their current service.

(4) Intangible Assets

Some companies have a distinct advantage over others due to their intangible assets, which include **patents, licenses, and brand recognition**. If a company establishes a well-known brand name, then it can charge a premium for its products or services. The perfect example might be Nike, which started out as a simple athletic-apparel company but has since become a major cultural institution and a purveyor not only of gear but of status. Designer fashion labels have similar business models, using their prestige to sell clothing for prices several times higher than the cost of production.

(5) Efficient Scale

When a niche market is effectively served by one or a small handful of companies, an efficient scale may be present. For example, midstream energy companies such as Enterprise Products Partners EPD enjoy a **natural geographic monopoly**. It would be too expensive to build a second set of pipes to serve the same routes; if a competitor tried this, it would cause returns for all participants to fall well below the cost of capital.

Findings from Morningstar Research[38] indicate that **not all moats are created equal**. Certain moat characteristics consistently lead to more

---

[38] Source: Morningstar "Not All Moats Are Created Equal" (3 Sept 2017)
https://www.morningstar.com/articles/823976/not-all-moats-are-created-equal

attractive financial performance than others. Let's see which ones tend to lead to more sustainable long-term financial outperformance.

Firm with Wide-Moat Far More Profitable Than Those with Narrow and/or No-Moat

EXHIBIT 1

Potent Profits Companies with wide moats are far more profitable than ones with narrow or no moats.

Fundamental Performance by Moat Rating Cohort

Moat Rating	Number of Companies	ROIC TTM (%)	ROIC Trailing 3 Yr (%)	ROIC Trailing 10 Yr (%)	Operating Margin Trailing 10 Yr (%)	Net Margin Trailing 10 Yr (%)
Wide	209	12.5	13.5	19.0	21.1	14.1
Narrow	643	9.0	9.7	14.8	14.7	9.0
None	651	5.1	4.8	8.6	7.6	4.4

All figures are medians.
Source: Morningstar. Data as of 05/16/2017.

Firms with Wide-Moat Tend to Outperform the Market

Morningstar's **Wide Moat** Focus Index[39] **outperformed** its Morningstar U.S. Market Index benchmark by 4.5% p.a. over a variety of market conditions, including boom and bust cycles in the commodity and housing markets.

---

[39] **Source: Morningstar "Economic Moats Matter: Here's the Evidence" (2 Sept 2017)** In 2007, Morningstar created the Wide Moat Focus Index based on the most undervalued wide-moat stocks in our coverage. To construct the index, we start with all U.S.-based and U.S.-traded companies to which we assign a wide moat rating (excluding master limited partnerships). We then select the cheapest stocks, as measured by the relationship of market price to Morningstar's estimate of fair value. The index consists of two subportfolios, each holding 40 stocks. The number of holdings that make it into the index depends on how many stocks are replaced when each subportfolio is reconstituted. Typically, the index holds about 50 stocks. The staggered reconstitution allows the index to hunt for undervalued stocks more frequently than a traditional semiannual reconstitution. It also aims to reduce total portfolio turnover. https://www.morningstar.com/articles/823977/economic-moats-matter-heres-the-evidence

Morningstar's record demonstrates the benefit of investing in stocks of **undervalued, high-quality businesses**. Performance attribution shows that **security selection** has **driven more than 98% of excess returns** for the Wide Moat Focus Index

---

EXHIBIT 1

Hefty Outperformance The Morningstar Wide Moat Focus Index consistently beat the market over the past 15 years.

	Trailing Annualized Total Return (%)				
	1-Year	3-Year	5-Year	10-Year	Inception 10/01/2002
Morningstar Wide Moat Focus Index	22.4	8.7	16.0	11.0	14.6
Benchmark: Morningstar US Market Index	12.4	8.5	14.6	7.2	10.1
Out/Underperformance vs. Benchmark	10.0	0.2	1.4	3.8	4.5

Source: Morningstar. Data as of 12/31/2016.

EXHIBIT 4

Through Boom and Bust The Wide Moat Focus Index performed well during a variety of market conditions, including boom and bust cycles in the commodity and housing markets.

Morningstar Wide Moat Focus Index — Morningstar US Market Index
— Morningstar Wide Moat Index — S&P 500

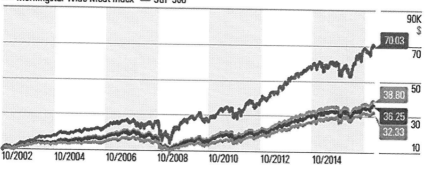

Source: Morningstar. All data 10/01/2002–12/31/2016. Official Benchmark: Morningstar US Market Index.

Source: Morningstar[40]

---

[40] Source: Morningstar "Economic Moats Matter: Here's the Evidence" (2 Sept 2017) https://www.morningstar.com/articles/823977/economic-moats-matter-her-es-the-evidence

Wide-Moat Firms Are More Likely to Benefit from Multiple Moat Sources Than Narrow- Moat Firms

Again, this is an intuitive result, as a **higher number of moat sources** should **lead to more-sustainable economic profits**. Morningstar's research indicates that **75% of wide-moat firms derive their competitive advantage from more than one moat source**, compared to just 60% of narrow-moat firms.

The most frequent moat source combination is **intangible assets and switching costs** (179 companies), followed closely by intangible assets and cost advantage (167 companies). The combination of the network effect and efficient scale is the least common by a wide margin (19 companies).

Firms That Benefit from Multiple Moat Sources Exhibit Better Fundamental Performance Than Those with Only One Moat Source.

This finding is intuitive as well. The **more barriers to entry** a company enjoys, the lower the risk that its competitive positioning will deteriorate and the **more sustainable its profitability**.

Network Effect Is the Most Likely to Drive a Wide Moat Rating.

Efficient Scale Is the Most Likely to Drive a Narrow Moat Rating.

When **efficient scale is cited as a moat source**, the associated company has been assigned a **narrow moat rating 88% of the time**. It becomes difficult to establish with a high degree of conviction that a company can still replicate its past performance over the subsequent 10 years.

Network effect leads to a wide moat rating for 37% of the companies to which it is applied, a higher frequency in percentage terms than any other moat source. This makes intuitive sense. **When a company establishes the network effect**, it can **often be a winner-take-all situation**, providing the **leading firm with a wide moat while leaving competitors with no moat at all**.

Consider the early days of social media when Facebook competed with Myspace. Although Myspace was at one time the most visited website in the United States, Facebook ultimately overtook it and is the dominant player, maintaining a wide moat rating. Myspace was acquired by News Corp for US$580 million in 2005 before being sold again for a reported US$35 million in 2011. Meanwhile, Facebook's market capitalization has since ballooned to roughly US$420 billion as of March 19, 2020.

Network Effect Drives Better Fundamental Performance Than Other Moat Sources Across Nearly Every Metric Examined.

As reflected in the following table, among the five potential moat sources, the cohort of companies that derive their competitive advantage from **network effect** has **posted the highest profitability** across every metric except trailing three-year returns on invested capital. This outcome reflects the fact that **although network effect is the least common moat source, it is very powerful once established**.

EXHIBIT 2

High Profitability Network effect drives better fundamental performance than other moat sources.

Fundamental Performance by Moat Source   ■ Top Performer ■ Bottom Performer

Moat Source	Number of Companies	ROIC TTM (%)	ROIC Trailing 3 Yr (%)	ROE TTM (%)	ROE Trailing 10 Yr (%)	Net Margin Trailing 10 Yr (%)
Network Effect	112	10.9	11.3	17.9	18.0	12.7
Intangible Assets	491	10.9	11.9	17.4	17.0	9.7
Switching Costs	314	10.4	10.8	15.1	16.0	10.8
Cost Advantage	358	9.8	11.1	14.7	16.2	9.9
Efficient Scale	200	7.4	7.3	11.9	12.5	10.4

All figures are medians
Source: Morningstar. Data as of 05/16/2017.

Additional Conclusions

In addition, Morningstar's Research observes that **wide-moat firms trade at the highest price/earnings ratios**, are the **least shorted**, have the **highest market caps**, and offer the lowest dividend yields.

Narrow-moat firms offer the highest growth. **No-moat firms trade at the lowest P/E**, offer the lowest growth, are the **most shorted**, have the **lowest market caps**, and offer the highest dividend yields.

Switching-cost firms trade at the lowest trailing five-year P/E. **Network-effect firms trade at the highest trailing and current P/E** (by far), **exhibit the highest growth**, and have the lowest dividend yields. Intangible-assets firms do not finish first or last on any metric. Cost-advantage firms have the highest market caps and are the least shorted. Efficient-scale firms trade at the lowest current P/E, have the lowest growth, are the most shorted, have the lowest market caps, and offer the highest dividend yields.

Ultimately, we **focus on companies with strong economic moats**, as they are **more likely to withstand their competitors and remain successful over the long run**.

Commitment No. 17

We look for businesses that have moats, especially if they have multiple moats, making their moats wider. We especially love businesses that have network effects.

QUICK SUMMARY

- An economic moat is company's ability to maintain a **competitive advantage** over its rivals
- Identify a **company's competitive advantage**: cost advantage, the network effect, high switching costs, intangible assets, efficient scale.
- Companies with **wide moats** are far more profitable than ones with narrow or no moat.
- Companies benefit from **multiple moat** sources.

CHAPTER 14

WHY DO WE INVEST IN BUSINESSES WITH HUGE TAILWINDS AND LARGE GROWING MARKETS

Total Addressable Market (TAM)

When we think about investing in the best businesses out there, we also want to make sure that these companies **have a sizable and growing total addressable market** (TAM) and the business can still further increase its market share.

We prefer to invest in companies that have the 3 Gs:

1) ✓ **Growing Business** (i.e. revenues, profitability & cash flows)
2) ✓ **Growing Total Addressable Market** (TAM)
3) ✓ **Growing Market Share**

Because **when these three Gs align**, the **businesses tend to get massive growth**. These are the businesses we would rather own anytime.

We **always prefer tailwinds** rather than headwinds:

1. **"Tailwinds"** refers to or describes a situation or condition that will **move growth, revenues, or profits higher**.
2. **"Headwinds"** are the opposite of the tailwinds. Headwinds in business are situations or conditions that **make growth harder**.

> *"The natural law of inertia: Matter will **remain at rest** or **continue in uniform in the same straight line** unless **acted upon by some external force**."*
> *- W. Clement Stone*

Growth in TAM / Growth in Market Share	Increasing Share of TAM	Decreasing Share of TAM
Growing TAM	✓	Depends
Declining TAM	✗	✗

We do not like to invest in companies that have the following 3 Ds:

4) ✗ **Declining Business** (i.e. revenues, margins, profits & cash flows)
5) ✗ **Declining Total Addressable Market** (TAM)
6) ✗ **Declining Market Share**

Declining = Slowing = Stagnating = Not Growing = Shrinking

We **do not like to invest in businesses that are struggling and shrinking**, and worst still, **in a market that is either not growing or shrinking**, and the business is **losing market share to other competitors**. The business will be on a downhill and gradually, revenues, profits, and cash flows will follow, and eventually, the share price will follow and move lower.

We **like inertia and momentum**. But we **like positive inertia and momentum even more**, not negative and slowing inertia. We **like to have tailwinds supporting our companies**, not tailwinds dragging them down.

Commitment No. 18

We love strong businesses that are growing, have strong tailwinds in growing markets, and are growing their market share.

Where Can You Find Information about the TAM?

Company's published annual reports, industry reports, etc.

We would like to share three examples where TAM is not static. It can be created, copied, and disrupted.

(1) Creating a new TAM

Let's look at how **Amazon** (then still an e-commerce company) came to **create Amazon Web Services (AWS) (cloud computing)** and in the process **creating a brand new TAM that the world never had** and **expanding their own TAM** in the result.

Amazon.com, Inc. (NASDAQ: AMZN) founded by Jeff Bezos in 1994, is a company focusing on e-commerce, cloud computing, digital streaming, and artificial intelligence. Amazon **initially started as an online marketplace for books**, but later **expanded to sell electronics, software, video games, apparel, furniture, food, toys, and jewelry** before becoming the **world's largest online marketplace** (basically everything).

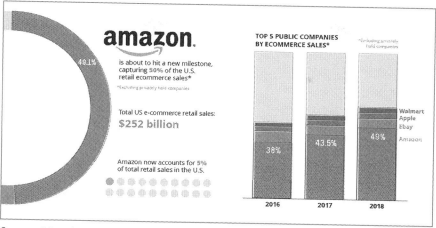

Source: Visual Capitalist[41]

Amazon's FY19 **Revenue was US$280bn, Operating Income was US$14.5bn**. However, Amazon Web Services (**AWS**), their cloud computing division, **accounted for US$35bn (12% of total revenues)** but had **US$9.2bn of operating income** (63.4% of total operating income, 26.3% operating profit margins)[42].

How did Amazon come to create a brand new business division outside of its core business (e-commerce) that **accounted for only 12% of revenues but close to 64% of operating profits?** AWS is definitely driving the bulk of Amazon's profitability,** especially in the last 5 years.

AWS started because Amazon's e-commerce business was growing so rapidly internally in 2003, they wanted to see how they **could expand Amazon's infrastructure, which was then being hosted in servers**. Amazon realized that this could have a lot of value to others potentially outside of Amazon and eventually **started selling it as infrastructure-as-a-service (IaaS)**.

---

[41] Source: Visual Capitalist https://www.visualcapitalist.com/chart-shows-amazons-dominance-ecommerce/
[42] Amazon FY19 10K Annual Report
https://ir.aboutamazon.com/static-files/63a014ac-bd47-42ce-b548-022a90d96e9a

AWS was first to market with a modern cloud infrastructure service when it launched Amazon Elastic Compute Cloud in August 2006. Surprisingly, it took several years before a competitor responded. As such, AWS managed to amass a larger market share. **Amazon AWS is now and still the market-leading IaaS public cloud computing company** and estimated by Gartner to have **close to 50% of the market share in 2018**, of a Worldwide IaaS Public Cloud Services **Market that grew +31.3%** in 2018[43].

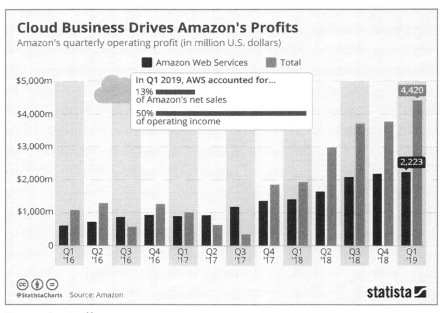

Source: Statista[44]

[43] Source: Gartner
"Gartner Says Worldwide IaaS Public Cloud Services Market Grew 31.3% in 2018" (29July2019) https://www.gartner.com/en/newsroom/press-releases/2019-07-29-gartner-says-worldwide-iaas-public-cloud-services-market-grew-31point3-per-cent-in-2018
[44] Statista: https://ir.aboutamazon.com/static-files/63a014ac-bd47-42ce-b548-022a90d96e9a

Worldwide IaaS Public Cloud Services Market Share, 2017-2018 (Millions of U.S. Dollars)

Company	2018 Revenue	2018 Market Share (%)	2017 Revenue	2017 Market Share (%)	2018-2017 Growth (%)
Amazon	15,495	47.8	12,221	49.4	26.8
Microsoft	5,038	15.5	3,130	12.7	60.9
Alibaba	2,499	7.7	1,298	5.3	92.6
Google	1,314	4.0	820	3.3	60.2
IBM	577	1.8	463	1.9	24.7
Others	7,519	23.2	6,768	27.4	11.1
Total	**32,441**	**100.0**	**24,699**	**100.0**	**31.3**

Source: Gartner (July 2019)

(2) Copy and Gaining Market Share from an Existing TAM

Let's look at Zoom Video Communications, Inc. ("ZM") as an example to illustrate.

> *Zoom is a video-first communications platform enabling frictionless video, voice, chat, and content sharing. Zoom enables face-to-face video experiences for thousands of people in a single meeting across disparate devices and locations. Zoom's cloud-native platform delivers reliable, high-quality video that is easy to use, manage and deploy, provides an attractive return on investment, is scalable and easily integrates with physical spaces and applications. Zoom's products include Zoom Meetings, Zoom Phone, Zoom Chat, Zoom Rooms, Zoom Conference Room Connector, Zoom Video Webinars, Zoom for Developers, and Zoom App Marketplace.*

Zoom is clearly not the first web-based meeting service provider, but clearly, they have zoomed their way to the top very rapidly with respect to video conferencing.

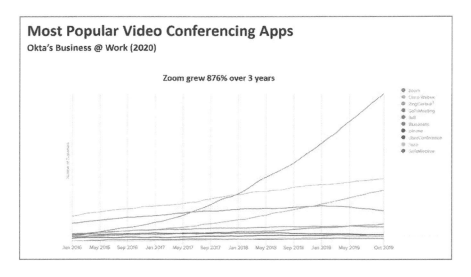

Most Popular Video Conferencing Apps
Okta's Business @ Work (2020)

Zoom grew 876% over 3 years

Zoom's Competition

Zoom primarily faces competition from:

1. ***Legacy web-based meeting providers***, *including* **Cisco Webex, LogMeIn,** *and* **GoToMeeting;**
2. ***Bundled productivity solutions providers with video functionality***, *including* **Microsoft Teams,** *and* **Google G Suite;** *and*
3. ***UCaaS and legacy PBX providers***, *including* **Avaya, RingCentral,** *and* **8x8***.*

But Zoom's market opportunity is sizeable at US$43bn in 2022.

Zoom's Market Opportunity

Video has increasingly become the way that individuals want to communicate in the workplace and their daily lives. As a result, it has become a fundamental component of today's communication and collaboration market, which also includes integrated voice, chat, and content sharing. IDC has defined this market as Unified Communications and Collaboration. Within this market, we address the Hosted

/ Cloud Voice and Unified Communications, Collaborative Applications and IP Telephony Lines segments. **IDC estimated that these segments combined represent a $43.1 billion opportunity in 2022**.

We believe **we address a broader opportunity than is currently captured in third-party market research** because once our customers begin to experience the benefits of our video-first communications platform, they tend **to greatly expand their use of video throughout their organizations.** As a result, we expect that use of our platform will significantly increase the penetration of video communications across a broad range of customer types and use cases. We believe that all of today's knowledge workers could benefit from our platform's ability to connect people through frictionless video, voice, chat, and content sharing.

Zoom's FY19 Revenue was US$330mil and growing rapidly +118%YoY

Zoom's Brief Financial Highlights

We believe that we have built a scalable and sustainable business model. We have thousands of customers of all sizes across industry verticals and geographies. We are experiencing rapid revenue growth and are generating positive cash flow from operations. Much of the primary capital that we have raised in recent years remains on our balance sheet, demonstrating the cash flow efficiency of our business. **Our revenue was $60.8 million, $151.5 million, $330.5 million, and $622 million** for the fiscal years ended January 31, **2017, 2018, 2019 and 2020**, respectively, representing annual revenue **growth of 149%, 118% and 88%** in fiscal 2018, 2019 and 2020, respectively. We had a net loss of $0.0 million and $3.8 million for the fiscal years ended January 31, 2017 and 2018, respectively, and net income of $7.6 million and $25.3 million for the fiscal year ended January 31,

2019. Cash provided by operations was $9.4 million, $19.4 million, $51.3 million, and $151.9 million for the fiscal years ended January 31, 2017, 2018, 2019 and 2020, respectively.

Source: Zoom Video Communications Form S-1 IPO Prospectus (Mar 2019)[45]

Zoom is listed as a **Leader in the 2019 Gartner Magic Quadrant for Meeting Solutions**. Second only to Cisco and on par with Microsoft.

Figure 1. Magic Quadrant for Meeting Solutions

Source: Gartner (September 2019)[46]

---

[45] Source: https://www.sec.gov/Archives/edgar/data/1585521/000119312519083351/d642624ds1.htm

[46] Source: https://zoom.us/gartner

Zoom believes they compete favorably based on the following competitive factors:

1. *Video-first platform;*
2. *Cloud-native architecture;*
3. *Functionality and scalability;*
4. *Ease of use and reliability;*
5. *Ability to utilize existing infrastructure, such as legacy conference room hardware; and*
6. *Low total cost of ownership*

Above is an example, Zoom's FY20 revenue is $622mil, growing rapidly at +88%YoY. There is no doubt growth will inevitably slow down over time, but the question at around 1.44% market share of the $43.1bn TAM, how big can Zoom grow to and continue to take market share?

(3) Disrupting existing TAM

Let's go through in greater detail how **Align Technology, Inc.** (NASDAQ: ALGN), founded in 1997, **disrupted the global metal braces market with invisible braces for teeth alignment.** ALGN is a global medical device company engaged in the design, manufacture, and marketing of **Invisalign clear aligners** and iTero intraoral scanners and services for orthodontics, and restorative and aesthetic dentistry.

Clear Aligner Treating Malocclusion (Misalignment of Teeth)

Malocclusion, or the misalignment of teeth, is **one of the most prevalent clinical dental conditions, affecting billions of people**, or **approximately 60% to 75% of the global population.**[47]

---

[47] Source: **Align Technology, Inc.** FY19 10K Annual Report
http://investor.aligntech.com/static-files/0fd246eb-ab75-4935-b70f-11a2b177ed9b

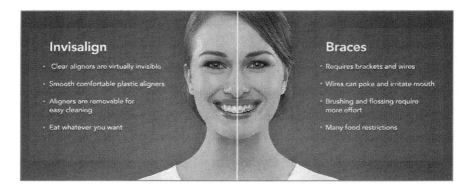

Annually, **approximately 12 million people** in major developed countries **elect treatment by orthodontists worldwide**. Most orthodontic patients are treated with the use of **traditional methods** such as **metal archwires and brackets**, referred to as **braces**, and may be augmented with elastics, metal expanders, headgear or functional appliances, and other ancillary devices as needed.

Upon completion of the treatment, the dental professional may, at his or her discretion, have the patient use a retainer appliance. Of the 12 million annual orthodontic cases started, Align **estimates that approximately 75% or 8.4 million could be treated using their Invisalign clear aligners**. In addition, approximately 300 million people with malocclusion could benefit from straightening their teeth.

The Invisalign System treats malocclusion based on a proprietary **computer-simulated virtual treatment plan** and a **series of doctor-prescribed, custom manufactured, clear plastic removable aligners**.

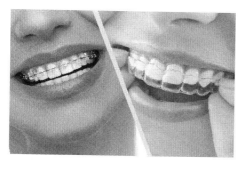

Growth in Invisalign Shipments since 2008

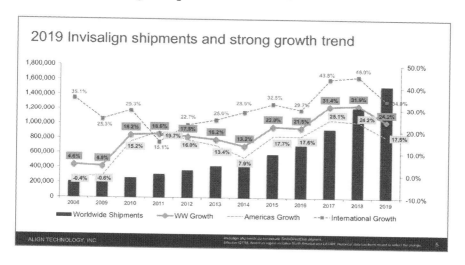

Align Technology's Management's 3 to 5 Year Financial Targets

3 to 5 year financial model targets

	Q4'18 Actual	Q3'19 Actual	Q4'19 Actual	3 – 5 Year Model
Annual Revenue Growth %	26.7%	20.2%	21.7%	20% - 30%
Gross Margin	71.7%	72.0%	72.6%	73% - 78%
Operating Expense %	49.2%	51.1%	49.4%	45% - 50%
Operating Margin	22.6%	20.9%	23.3%	25% - 30%
Free Cash Flow*	35.0%	34.2%	27.0%	20% - 25%

*Free cash flow is a non-GAAP measure defined as cash flow from operations less purchase of property, plant and equipment

ALIGN TECHNOLOGY, INC   41

Source: Align Technology's Q4 and Full Year 2019 Financial Slides[48]

Similar examples of disruption are also how Uber and Airbnb with technology, disrupted the industry with ride-hailing and home-sharing, thus providing these companies with an edge and efficient scale to an otherwise existing competitive market.

These three examples (Amazon, Zoom Video Communications, and Align Technology) are provided to give you a flavor to illustrate that TAM is never static. TAM is always evolving and can always be created, copied, and/or disrupted. We prefer to invest in companies with the three Gs that have a **growing business** in a **growing TAM** and are **growing market share**.

QUICK SUMMARY

- **Invest in companies with the 3 Gs**: Growing business, growing total addressable market (TAM), growing market share.
- Choose **tailwinds over headwinds**. Tailwinds move growth, revenue, or profits higher.
- Total addressable market (TAM) can be **created, copied, or disrupted**.

---

[48] ALGN Q4 and Full Year 2019 Financial Slides
http://investor.aligntech.com/static-files/54ca8bd7-6ea0-458c-8129-1e5889a4fadb

CHAPTER 15

WHAT DO WE USE AS A FRAMEWORK TO FIND GREAT BUSINESSES?

Focus on the Long-Term, Not the Short-Term

Because for us individual investors, most of the advice we get from **financial media and advisors** is the **exact opposite** of what we should be doing when it comes to investing. Because **their goals often are not your goals**, their outlook tends to **revolve around the fees they charge** (how much money can they make from you this month and next month?), their **short-term thinking**, and their lack of transparency. The so-called "wise" are obsessed with what's happening by the **short-term noise**, minute-by-minute, hour-by-hour, day-by-day. How is the market doing today, up or down? What did the Fed do? What is stock ABC moving after its earnings? What do the elections mean for next quarter?

It is all **so incredibly short-term**, against the **very antithesis of how we should be investing**. The vast majority of wealth is built in the public markets for people who want staying power, who want to build wealth over decades, not over a couple of weeks (to consistently do that is close to impossible). **Businesses** are already building long-term wealth, to achieve the same goal, you have to **ride with them over these long periods of time**.

You have to **find the right culture, strategies, and businesses** to do so. A business that has built, for example, a culture of proven innovation **will continue to churn out positive results and corresponding profits** long after it misses analysts' expectations by EPS $0.02 in a specific quarter. Thus, you need to realize and focus on the **importance of focusing on and holding the stock before we decide how to buy a stock**. Because if your mindset is wrong, and even if you discover all the best companies that are likely to outperform, you will almost surely self-sabotage yourself into failure.

Find, Invest, and Hold Your Winners

Recall the mathematics we discussed in the earlier chapters: **Mathematically the worst thing you can do as an investor is to lose any of your big winners**. If you buy a stock, there is always the chance you could lose 100% of your investment. Though it is unlikely that the company will go bankrupt, there is a chance. But while on the **downside**, your **losses are capped at max -100%**, on the **upside,** there is **no limit (>>100%) to your gains** as to how much your investments can increase in value. Look at some of these stocks in the following chart; they have increased by more than +1000% over many years. What eventually happens is that **after some years, 20% of your winners will end up contributing 80% of your gains**, and **your losers will fade into obscurity** and account for an insignificant part of your investment portfolio. In fact, more likely than not you will find that **the gains from your largest single winner** can **more than offset all the losses from all your losers**.

Let's look at the 9 stocks below for example over different charts starting from January 1, 2006:

In the first year, it is usually all over the place. You have some winners and some losers.

One-Year Chart

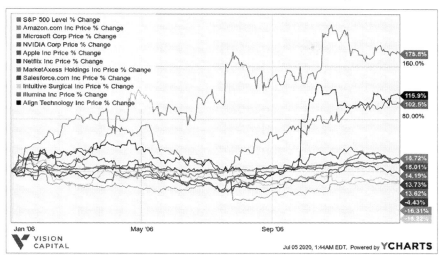

Source: YCharts January 1, 2006 – December 31, 2006

In five years, some massive winners are starting to appear. You might still have some losers that underperform the market.

Five-Year Chart

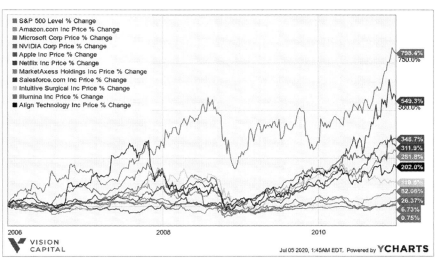

Source: YCharts January 1, 2006 – December 31, 20

Now, in a **ten-year** horizon, these winners are starting to really fly. You still have a bunch of market-beating business and some losers.

Ten-Year Chart

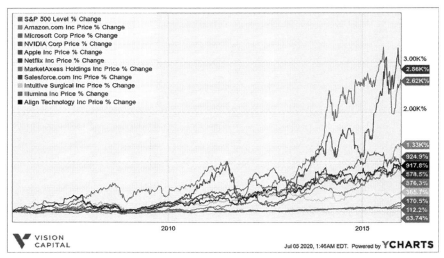

Source: YCharts January 1, 2006 – December 31, 2015

Now, in a **fifteen-year** chart, these massive winners just fly even more. Unexpectedly most of the companies are actually beating the market. Woohoo!

Fifteen-Year Chart

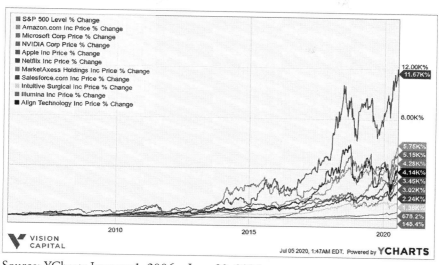

Source: YCharts January 1, 2006 – June 30, 2020

This is what we have experienced when we invest in the strongest companies; these charts are really meant to provide you a feeling of what we went through. **Because winners always win, and the best winners win even bigger**.

Thus, **if you miss a few monster investments, those multibaggers**[49] as Peter Lynch referred to them, it does not matter how many times you save a couple of percentage points by selling a stock on its way down. **You will never catch up to the gains you missed out on had you stayed committed to the ones that eventually become your great winners**. A better approach is to **find great businesses** and **add money regularly to them over time**. That's the way we think about investing, and that is your best path to lasting wealth.

---

[49] A multibagger stock is an equity stock which gives a return of more than 100%. The term was coined by Peter Lynch in his 1988 book, "One Up on Wall Street" and comes from baseball where "bags" or "bases" that a runner reaches are the measure of the success of a play. For example, a ten bagger is a stock which gives returns equal to 10 times the investment, while a twenty-bagger stock gives a return of 20 times.

Countless times, you heard many investors complain, "**If only I held….**" or "**If only I had bought …**". You need to not underestimate what your itchy trigger fingers can do. You need to realize that 25% p.a. investment returns is not just 23% p.a. ahead of what you can get on bank deposits but can turn you into millionaires many times over. If you are **focused on the short-term, you would have missed that great business story** and the riches that came with it for committed investors.

There are **thousands and thousands of public companies**, and **many of these will do poorly as investments**. But the ones that end up being multibaggers? You do not want to trade your way out of those. That is **why a long-term patient approach is a defining feature of how we invest**.

This is the framework that we have built and refined over the last couple of years and are still using it to this very day. We use these tenets to determine whether or not a company meets my investing criteria for us to even take a closer look and to allocate our capital to it. The **companies and businesses that we own** are **companies that we view as the world's greatest investments for the long-term. We aim to crush the market** as we **hold** these stocks **for a minimum of five years**.

You will realize subsequently that **we will not even attempt to cover valuation**. We do not do complicated discounted cash flow (DCF) valuations and we are **not concerned with short-term earnings misses/hits** by EPS $0.01 or **with 12-month price targets**. That is not a space we are in and want to be in, and that makes us different from probably 99% of the investors out there.

We will start with a brief overview and then spend more time to explain what we mean and what we look for in each pillar. We **will be naming companies and leaders that we admire and invest in**. To add one caveat, **things do not always go according to plan**, so it is possible that some of the companies and individuals might have hit on rough times by the time you read these pages. That's a danger of publishing and of investing; **we don't know what we don't know**. But we have to content ourselves with making the best decisions based on the information we have.

Four Pillars of Vision Investing -

(1) Substantial Business Opportunity (Strategy)

- ✓ The top dog and first mover in an important, growing, and emerging industry that is innovative and forward-thinking and will change the world and shape our future for the better. Revenues that are small in relation to a large and/or growing market.
- ✓ Large expanding global market opportunity. Revenues that are large in a fast-growing market.
- ✓ Strong business strategy & supports clear and sustainable competitive advantages
- ✓ Increasing predictable and/or sustainable pricing power
- ✓ Passes the Snap Test (if business disappears now, would it make a difference?)
- ✓ Maintains an element of evident optionality

(2) Promising Financial Performance (Financials)

- ✓ Large market opportunity with excellent reinvestment economics
- ✓ Sales growth greater than or accelerating towards 20%
- ✓ Strong stable/rising profitability or improving profitability and returns on capital (reflects operating leverage and pricing power, competitive advantage)
- ✓ Scalable business model that supports or will support growing cash flows
- ✓ Strong and worry-free balance sheet (preferably net cash with little or no debt)
- ✓ Access to capital to fund high rates of growth indefinitely
- ✓ Strong past price appreciation and have outperformed the market
- ✓ Grossly overvalued according to the financial media

(3) Visionary Leadership & Strong Management (Management)

- ✓ Founder-led or Founder is still involved
- ✓ CEO has a large, expansionist vision and is likely to remain for at least 5 to 10 years

- ✓ Key executives own at least 5% of shares
- ✓ Executive compensation is closely aligned with shareholders
- ✓ Leadership has a track record of outperformance, integrity, capability, and an innovative mindset.

(4) High-quality Culture (Culture)

- ✓ High Glassdoor ratings and reviews for CEO and employee
- ✓ Leadership maintains a culture of high performance and low turnover
- ✓ High quality of directors and Board members

Four Types of Companies We Invest in

1. Titans of Industry

These are the **gargantuan, unstoppable businesses** that **despite their size** ($100+ billion market cap) — **are leading the way and are still shaping the future**. These are typically big companies with lots of resources at their disposal. Some of them might pay dividends and have rock-solid financials. Given their competitive positions and available resources, the risk is naturally much lower. Yes, sometimes **the big can still get bigger**, and we're on the hunt for these ambitious companies.

2. Proven Winners

We think these companies — which **lead large and growing industries** — are Titans in the making and slowly shaping the future and the world in which we live in. They are smaller than the Titans but still possess many of the traits we look for in good businesses. With **proven track records, strong competitive advantages, compelling business models, and growth potential**, there's plenty of outperformance left to grab.

3. Emerging Stars

These **mid-cap** players **have proven** they **have what it takes to scale** and are **still relatively early in their long-term journey**. Although the risk can be a bit higher with larger and proven companies, we believe these companies **hold a winning strategy** and a **long runway ahead** of them.

4. Moonshots

These **(relatively) small companies** — these **dynamic companies are still in the early stages of disrupting and shaping their industries, businesses, economies and even our daily lives** — **have notable risk but asymmetric upside.** They **have a lot of promise** but given their size, market, or even valuation are simply riskier investments. They tend to be working toward meaningful profitability. This category's **accuracy will likely be lower** as these companies still have to **prove themselves in competitive industries,** but **one big winner is all we need to dramatically boost our portfolio's outperformance.**

Rule Makers	Titans of the Industry
Rule Makers	Proven Winners
Rule Breakers	Emerging Stars
Rule Breakers	Moonshots

QUICK SUMMARY

- **Ignore financial media**; their goals are not your goals.
- **Find, invest and hold your winners.**
- **Invest in titans of the industry, proven winners, emerging stars, and moonshots.**

CHAPTER 16

WHY SUBSTANTIAL BUSINESS OPPORTUNITY (STRATEGY) AND HOW DO WE LOOK FOR IT?

Top Dog and First Mover in an Important and Emerging Industry

We are looking for **top dogs who are rule-makers, first movers, and rule-breakers**. Top dogs tend to hold the dominant market share in the industry, and often they are the largest by market capitalization. First movers tend to be the innovators that are first to exploit a niche, essentially creating its market. And finally, that niche must be worth dominating.

Some rule-breaking companies that have become rule makers are **Google** (internet search provider), **Facebook** and Instagram (social media), **Netflix** (streaming entertainment), **Salesforce.com** (customer relationship management, CRM), **Amazon** (e-commerce and cloud computing), **Visa and Mastercard** (electronic payments) and **Microsoft** (software and cloud computing).

There is also Starbucks in coffee. Starbucks did not invent the cafe or coffee shop. But they were the **first to conceive of these businesses on a national and ultimately international scale when others did not see the growth opportunity**.

There are emerging industries all around us: robotics, automation, cloud computing, virtual reality, artificial intelligences, and many others. These companies are not hidden; they are right there before our eyes, bringing disruptive technology, clever and effective marketing, or a brand-new business model.

There are plenty of factors to analyze when evaluating the strategic land-scape for a company, we focus on four key things:

1. Does the business have **pricing power?**
2. What is the business's **sustainable competitive advantage?**
3. What is the size of the business versus its **market opportunity?**
4. What is the level of **loyalty** of its **customer base?**

(1) Pricing Power: Why Do We Look for It?

Warren Buffett's **top factor for his greatest performing investments is pricing power**: understanding a **company's ability to manage its pricing over time**. His greatest investments like Coca-Cola and American Express were able to raise prices sustainably, and with staying power, over long periods and that **created a compounding machine**.

Because when a company can raise prices, they often can invest in scale in operations and technology, gaining even more marginal benefit from their pricing strategies. That's why pricing power is one of the leading factors. We ask ourselves:

1. Can the company **afford** to raise prices?
2. How **predictable** is it?
3. How **sustainable** is it?

You **do not have a lot of pricing power if you are selling a commoditized product that somebody buys** (be it frequently or infrequently). A company that more commonly forms pricing power by creating a habit - a reliance on future repeat purchases without blinking twice at the price. With its ubiquity, along with the consistency and quality of the experience, Starbucks has some proven pricing power.

Note that we said "some." Starbucks does not have to double their prices because that will likely create some outage. But if Starbucks increases prices by $0.20 - $0.40 here and there every now and then, we are likely okay. That will make a massive difference to their financials versus their competitors.

So, we are looking for businesses that have the ability to raise prices steadily. We ask ourselves when we buy something: **"What would I have been willing to pay for that? What would I pay more?"**

Other examples:

> Would you pay more for **Netflix**? Netflix faces competition from traditional cable TV, Amazon, HBO, Disney, and other challengers along with many international first movers. But considering that Netflix is expanding its product offerings so much more than anyone else and has the vast consumer data to feed its recommendation engine to enrich our viewing experience, that's worth more to me.

> This is not that different from **Spotify** as well, where I play all my music whenever and whatever I want. The amount I pay a month to have my playlists downloaded to my phone, play any music both new and old, and not have to spend countless hours searching and downloading it is absolutely fun.

> Speaking of **Amazon**, how about **Amazon Prime**? We know many people would not even second guess paying a

few more dollars more for their Prime membership, which comes with free delivery and entertainment.

A **Costco membership**. The unique Costco shopping experience and the dirt-cheap prices keep the company's membership retention numbers strong. Costco customers are extremely loyal.

(2) Sustainable Competitive Advantage: Why Do We Look for It?

Pricing power often reflects the sustainable advantage that a business has. Successful businesses attract competition. The critical question is how well a company can fend off that competition.

In some businesses, like the **pharmaceutical industry**, **patents** can enforce a lasting competitive advantage. On the other hand, patent protection can be problematic in the software industry, where patented inventions can often be worked around. Luckily, there are other ways of protecting a competitive advantage.

Companies have **trade secrets** (the formula for Coke is not patented, just a well-guarded secret) and they can build expertise that others find hard to duplicate. Some businesses require daunting levels of capital investment to establish (e.g. pharmaceutical companies), while others invest in their **reputation** and **brand names** (e.g. Nike, Adidas, etc.).

Sometimes a company's leaders are just smarter than the competition, and sometimes these competitors just fail to adapt to the changing world. The **key** is to what we call a **company's moat or competitive advantage**, their protection against inevitable competitors, and to find out how many competitors are in it.

We want and we demand the companies we invest in to have a sustainable competitive advantage either gained through business momentum, patent protection, visionary leadership, or inept competitors. Because **if they have**

little to no competitive advantage, competitors will be able to come in easily and beat them. These are definitely not the companies we want to be looking at.

Let's look at some examples:

Business Momentum

Amazon was one of the pioneers in online commerce, starting out as an online bookseller **before expanding its reach into...pretty much anything you can imagine**. Its visionary founder and leader, Jeff Bezos, always intended Amazon to be more than just books, and he quickly moved the company into movies and DVDs, and then nearly anything and everything anyone one needs. Amazon built customer relationships and success so quickly that it became a retailing force. That real business momentum has carried Amazon to become one of the most amazing success stories in commerce history.

Patent Protection

This trait is the most reliant on government protection, so it's probably our least favorite, but it's still important. **Biotech and drug companies** come to our minds, as do many **tech companies**. This is especially true for companies that design intellectual property that goes inside our iPhones, laptops, televisions, or connected cars. **Chip companies** are another example.

Visionary Leadership

Steve Jobs, Mark Zuckerberg, and Jeff Bezos. Not every leader is a visionary, some are more operations-driven. And that's important too. But true Rule Breaker companies (as opposed to Rule Fakers) are led by strategic visionaries who have their hearts and souls (if not their bank accounts, through stock ownership) tied to their company's success.

Inept Competition

Netflix comes to mind as a perfect example. In its early days, Netflix completely disrupted the movie rental industry by providing online DVD rentals. With Blockbuster basically not doing anything and providing no competition, Netflix managed to become the largest streaming entertainment in the U.S. and growing internationally rapidly.

(3) Market Size: Why Do We Look for It?

The second factor we look at is the **size of the market opportunity**. You can be investing in a thriving business, but they were running out of room to attract new customers. The ultimate market size just was not there. And if the pie is static, or worse, shrinking, then a five- or ten-year investing time frame really does not matter at all.

Take a snowboard company for example, even if the company had great culture, a founder CEO, solid financials, and even if it was the snowboard king, how many customers might there be? How many snowboards do people own? How often do people snowboard? How many places to snowboard are there?

So really it is not just about the market size for a company. We **need to see that management is smart about grabbing more of it.** For example, when Starbucks first started it was just U.S.-focused, and they were clearly saturating and maximizing the number of its store locations in the U.S. with nowhere left to grow. That's when Howard Schultz and his team went abroad. There are now more than ten thousand Starbucks stores outside the U.S. and growing. International stores now account for more than 40% of total stores growing at +20% YoY and close to 30% of revenues. This is versus same-store growth for the U.S. growing at +5% YoY. They also moved to licensing, which now accounts for close to half of all of their stores.

When a company **knows its customers and moves aggressively to identify new market opportunities, enlarging it, and then capturing it,** these are truly the best companies because of the **long runway of growth**. That is truly what we look at when we consider market size.

These companies can be either **solving old problems** or **inventing new possibilities**. We want to be seeking growth in dynamic companies that are **disrupting and shaping industries, businesses, economies, and even our daily lives**. Some of which you might know well and others entirely unfamiliar.

What they **have all in common** is a **desire to keep innovating and delighting** and to **create products and services** that **truly change the world for the better** and **shape our future**.

Ultimately, we focus on the future, and we love investing in companies with great businesses, with visionary leaders making bold strategic decisions that lead to ever-higher growth in sales, profits, and cash flows.

> *"Changing the world never does happen overnight.*
> *And neither do multibaggers."*
> *- David Gardner*

Total Addressable Market (TAM): How Do We Look for It?

Assessing these three factors (pricing power, market opportunity, and customer loyalty) is as much art as science. There are numbers you can pull together **from online research** or **from a company** (IPO Prospectus Form S-1, annual reports, investor presentations) in the form of **total addressable market (TAM)**.

Let us go through an example of the TAM figures from **online research for Alphabet (i.e. Google)** and **Facebook** that we managed to pull out with a simple Google search:

> *Digital Ad Spending as % of Total Media Ad Spending is only going to keep increasing. Of which a **large part of it will go to the Duopoly of Google (search) and Facebook***

(social media). WARC in its Global Advertising Trends Report[50] estimates that **Google and Facebook's share of the global online ad market will grow to 61.4% in 2019, up from 56.4%** *in 2018 (winners win). The duopoly's US$176.4 billion in forecasted ad revenues amounts to a* **+22% increase versus 2018**. *For everyone else, the future looks tough as internet advertising spend outside the duopoly is predicted to fall by -7.2%.*

Below Is an Example of Global and U.S. Digital Ad Spend (online research)

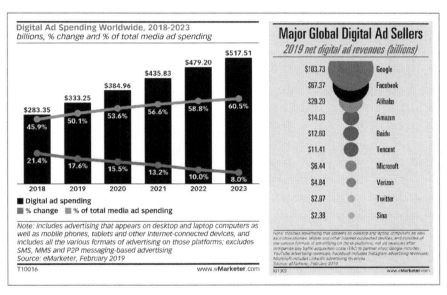

[50] Source: https://www.raconteur.net/business-innovation/google-facebook-duopoly

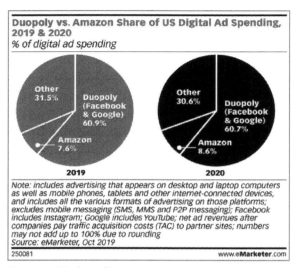

Duopoly vs. Amazon Share of US Digital Ad Spending, 2019 & 2020
% of digital ad spending

2019

Other 31.5%
Duopoly (Facebook & Google) 60.9%
Amazon 7.6%

2020

Other 30.6%
Duopoly (Facebook & Google) 60.7%
Amazon 8.6%

Note: includes advertising that appears on desktop and laptop computers as well as mobile phones, tablets and other internet-connected devices, and includes all the various formats of advertising on those platforms; excludes mobile messaging (SMS, MMS and P2P messaging); Facebook includes Instagram; Google includes YouTube; net ad revenues after companies pay traffic acquisition costs (TAC) to partner sites; numbers may not add up to 100% due to rounding
Source: eMarketer, Oct 2019

250081   www.eMarketer.com

Source: eMarketer[51]

With the duopoly and strong market position (we would watch Amazon though) and disruption to the traditional ad spend away to digital, **one should not be surprised to see Google and Facebook continue to dominate and keep growing revenues over time** with the **tailwind is in their favor.**

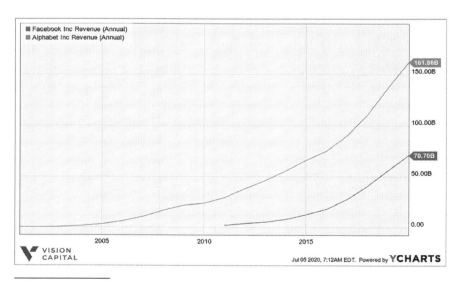

■ Facebook Inc Revenue (Annual)
■ Alphabet Inc Revenue (Annual)

161.86B
150.00B
100.00B
70.70B
50.00B
0.00

2005   2010   2015

VISION CAPITAL

Jul 05 2020, 7:12AM EDT. Powered by YCHARTS

[51] Source: eMarketer
https://www.emarketer.com/content/facebook-google-duopoly-won-t-crack-this-year

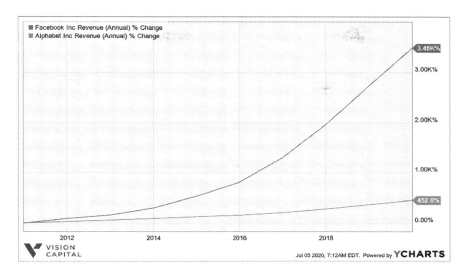

Below is an example of the **Total Addressable Market (TAM)** provided by Uber Inc in their IPO Prospectus Form S-1.

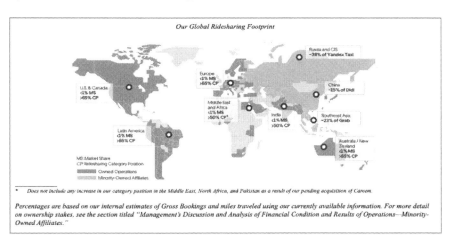

Our Market Opportunity

We address a massive opportunity in powering movement from point A to point B. The scope of our bold mission, unparalleled size of our global network, and breadth of our platform offerings lead to a very large market opportunity for us. We view our market opportunity in terms of a total addressable market ("TAM"), which we believe that we can address over the long-term, and a serviceable addressable market ("SAM"), which we currently address. As of the quarter ended December 31, 2018, we had Ridesharing operations in 63 countries with an aggregate population of 4.1 billion people. For additional information regarding our estimates and calculations, see the section titled "Market, Industry, and Other Data."

Personal Mobility

Our Personal Mobility TAM consists of 11.9 trillion miles per year, representing an estimated $5.7 trillion market opportunity in 175 countries. We include all passenger vehicle miles and all public transportation miles in all countries globally in our TAM, including those we have yet to enter, except for the 20 countries that we address through our ownership positions in our minority-owned affiliates, over which we have no operational control other than approval rights with respect to certain material corporate actions. We estimate that these 20 countries represent an additional estimated market opportunity of approximately $0.5 trillion.

Our current Personal Mobility SAM consists of 3.9 trillion miles per year, representing an estimated $2.5 trillion market opportunity in 57 countries. We include only these 57 countries in our SAM as they are the countries where we operate today, other than the six countries identified below where we experience significant regulatory restrictions. We also include all miles traveled in passenger vehicles for trips under 30 miles in our SAM. We do not include miles from trips greater than 30 miles, as the vast majority of our trips are shorter than this distance. While we believe that a portion of our trips can be a substitute for public transportation, we exclude public transportation miles from our SAM given the price differential between the two modes of transportation.

We plan to grow our current SAM by expanding further into our six near-term priority countries, Argentina, Germany, Italy, Japan, South Korea, and Spain, where our ability to grow our Ridesharing operations to scale is currently and may continue to be limited by significant regulatory restrictions. We already offer certain Personal Mobility products such as livery vehicles, taxi partnerships, and dockless e-bikes in several of these countries, and hope to grow our presence in these six countries in the near future to the extent regulatory restrictions are reduced. For trips under 30 miles, we estimate that these six countries account for 0.8 trillion vehicle miles. We calculate the market opportunity of these 0.8 trillion vehicle miles to be $0.5 trillion. We refer to this opportunity, together with our current SAM, as our near-term SAM. Our near-term SAM consists of 4.7 trillion miles per year, representing an estimated $3.0 trillion market opportunity in 63 countries. We believe that we are just getting started: consumers only traveled approximately 26 billion miles on our platform in 2018, implying a less than 1% penetration rate of our near-term SAM.

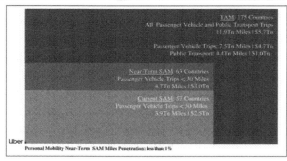

Source: Uber Inc IPO Prospectus Form S-1

Another source of research often overlooked is **YouTube videos** and **quarterly analyst earnings conference calls**. Search any of the leadership names (primarily CEO and CFO) for online speeches or talks they have given, and you will often find fabulous insights into the company's strategy, directly from the individuals responsible for setting that strategy.

(4) Consumer Loyalty: Why Do We Look for It?

The successful investor Bernard Baruch was once asked at a party for some stock picks. Rather than share his favorite ticker, he explained his simple methodology for finding winning investments—one that I have embraced as well. **"Find companies whose products you buy, use, throw away, or however you have used it, you need to repurchase it within 30 days."**

Customers are creatures of habit. Start with your own experiences, then extend it to the companies that you are looking at.

1. Are the customers going back?
2. Are they even spending more the next time?
3. Are they buying other products?

Basically, we want to see if the customers are going repeatedly to spend more and more dollars. **We like businesses that generate repeat purchases, are recurring in nature, and with deepening relationships with its customers.**

Put these three factors together and you will find:

A company with pricing power with a large and growing market opportunity whose customers are enthusiastically going there repeatedly because it is the best place to find what they want or need.

Overall Strategy: What Do We Look for?

1. **Companies with pricing power** - the ability to successfully raise prices over time, often reflected by increasing gross margins over three to five years.
2. **Businesses that serve growing, dynamic markets with years of expansion ahead** of them.
3. A **business model built on repeat purchases or recurring revenues**.
4. A **track record for capital allocation** that suggests long-term shareholder success with limited asset write-downs or charges against earnings.
5. A company that has **created or is transforming a niche business that has lots of growth ahead.**

Businesses with **all of these factors** should become multibagger winners in the long run.

We really need all of these factors. You can have some if not most, but what we have seen is that businesses with all of these tend to really thrive and keep growing and expand, and that's what we want to be invested in for the long term.

In either case, even though a business can be profitable, if the **upside to further growth is only going to be limited to a static / shrinking/niche market**, then there is **only a limited upside** to how much the business can scale and grow.

Similarly, even if the business is in a rapidly growing market with lots of expansion opportunities, if the **business model itself is not profitable** and is struggling with pricing power and revenue is lumpy and not recurring, the **business will likely not be able to last for long**.

Overall Strategy: How Do We Look for It?

Read the company's annual report. We make it a point to always at least read through the entire annual report because it will clearly detail many things that traditional financial media will not be able to tell you.

Think about these questions and try to answer it as you are reading it:

1) Is the **business growing** in terms of revenues? Or stable or declining?

2) Are **profitability and profits rising**? Or stable or declining?

3) Does the business reflect some sort of **pricing power**? Gross margin expansion?

4) Are **cash flows** (OCF and FCF) **positive, increasing, and growing faster** than revenues as the business expands? Is this

sustainable? If not positive, is there a **trend in improving cash flow dynamics**?

5) What are the **competitive advantages** of the business?

6) What is the **business model**? How does the business **make their money**? Which parts of the business are growing faster than others? What is the percentage split? Is it sustainable? What are the trends telling? Is the business strategy geared towards it?

7) Are there **repeat purchases** from customers? And customers are **coming back to buy even more**? What is the Net Dollar Retention Rate (NBRR) if it is available?

8) Is the **customer count increasing**? Are customers **satisfied** and being delighted? Are customers loyal and celebrating the company's brand? Do you think customers are willing to pay more? What is the net promoter score (NPS)?

9) Are the **revenues recurring** based on long term sales contracts or repeat purchases?

10) Who are their customers? Is there a concentration risk? What are they doing to expand the business? Can they expand further still?

11) How does the business **acquire new customers and upset existing customers**? Are **sales and marketing efficient and effective**? Is management using the best strategy?

12) What is the **total addressable market (TAM)** for the business? Is TAM **expanding and growing**? Is this an **existing market or a newly disrupted market**? What is their **market share and is it growing**?

13) How is the company doing against its **competitors**? Are they gaining market share? Are they the **leader** and **disruptor**? Is the company **innovative**?

14) Does management have a **clear growth strategy**? Have they had **successful track records**?

15) How does the business **spend its money**? Is there operating leverage such that expenses (e.g. S&M, R&D, G&A) can fall as a percentage of revenues as the business expands? Are expenses increasing at a slower rate compared to revenue growth? Are these falling through to a rise in net income and net income margins?

16) If the business is **still in expansion**, how is the company **allocating capital**? How are they thinking about it? Is it internally-generated R&D or via external acquisitions? Are acquisitions successfully integrated?

17) **How are they going to fund it**? Do they have sufficient capital? Is there smart use of debt and equity to enhance shareholder returns?

Above are some questions that we have thought of. Undeniably, there can be a lot more; we would love for you to continue adding to this list as your knowledge (and circle of competence) expands. We love thinking about the businesses we own for the long term this way because we grow smarter along with them on this journey.

Summary: Strategy Checklist

1. Evidence of pricing power
2. A stable, ideally expanding, long term gross profit margins, EBIT, EBITDA, and Net Income margins.
3. Evidence of repeat purchase and with more products and higher spent.
4. A "brand flock," customers who are not only loyal but also celebrate the company's brand.
5. An addressable market that's growing
6. Evidence that acquisitions are successfully integrated.
7. Smart use of debt and equity to enhance shareholder returns

8. A management team that is clear about its growth strategy and has a successful past.

QUICK SUMMARY

- We look for **top dogs who are rule-makers**, **first movers, and rule-breakers.**
- Consider a company's pricing power, its **ability to manage its pricing over time**.
- Look for companies with **sustainable competitive advantage**.
- A company's **market opportunity** matters.
- **Consumer loyalty** is a key indicator of a business's success.

CHAPTER 17

WHY FINANCIALS AND WHAT DO WE LOOK FOR?

Why Sales Growth?

We have gone back and done some historical research on the **best-performing stocks over the past twenty-five years**, and our **conclusion** is that the **number one factor** was <u>high rates of sales growth</u>.

In other words, you don't end up with a twenty-bagger because that company was growing its top line at 5% per year. Because if top-line growth is not there, there will be limits as to how much the company can keep growing earnings with expanding profit margins (yes there is probably a ceiling). Don't get us wrong, there is absolutely nothing wrong with 5% annual revenue growth rates. There are wonderful companies that grow at twice the level of GDP growth, but they usually do not end up delivering multibagger returns for their investors.

Top dogs grow their top lines. Period. The companies that end up being the **twenty, thirty or forty-baggers** are the ones that will change the course of your portfolio and grow your wealth from $50,000 into $700,000 (or from $300,000 into $4 million), **all have very strong customer demand and very strong sales growth.**

Here's a telling fact we learned when we researched **Starbucks and Costco**. Since they went public more than twenty-five years ago, the **sales growth for both companies outpaced their stock price growth** (see the following two charts). The two stocks have gone up between 15-25% per year for almost 25 years, and those rates of returns are astonishing. But their sales have grown even faster! It is also similar for **Alphabet** (see third chart).

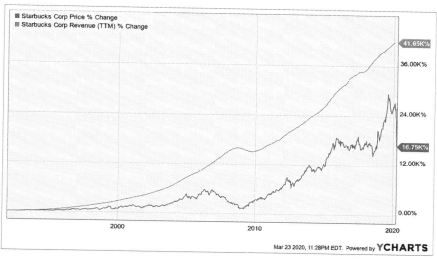

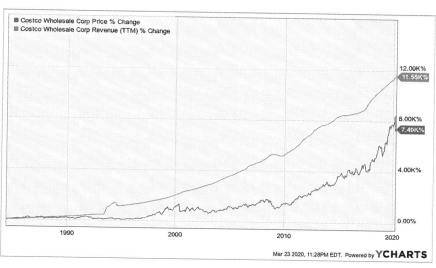

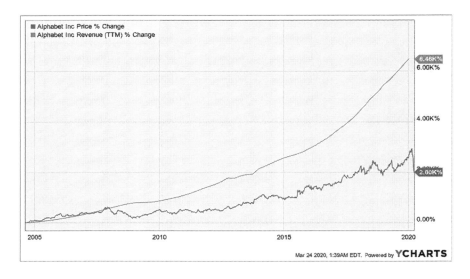

So, we **like to find sales growth,** and I get really excited when I find one. In our dream scenario, in particular, we are **finding high and accelerating sales growth.** It will be a **challenge to find because of the law of large numbers.** Because eventually, sales growth will decline once sales become too massive and the company becomes a top dog with the largest market share.

Why Returns of Capital? Why Earnings?

If we go back to the late 1990s during the burst of the dot com bubble, we had some incredible sales-growth stories that went bankrupt because these companies were burning through so much cash. So, **sales growth alone is not sufficient if profits and cash flow do not come along with it.** Even if you have massive volumes and revenues, but **no profits and no cash, the company will not last indefinitely.** That we are certain. Thus, the company should be **profitable or if not yet profitable,** have demonstrated some sort of **path towards improving profitability.**

We **especially like rising and improving profit margins and especially when the business has operating leverage** because that means the business has operating leverage. For example, for every $1 of revenue, it spends even less on expenses and generates more profits:

1) **Cost of Goods** —> Gross Profit Margins
2) **R&D** Expense —> EBITDA, EBIT, and Net Income Margins
3) **S&M** Expense —> EBITDA, EBIT, and Net Income Margins
4) **G&A** Expense —> EBITDA, EBIT, and Net Income Margins

We like to **find high rates of return on invested capital** and smart alloca-tion decisions. As a general number, we look for returns on equity (ROE) of at least 10%, with manageable debt levels. This means every dollar invested in the business returns at least $0.10 back. 10% is about average for most US companies so ideally, we are looking higher for businesses that are gen-erating 15%, 20%, or more in ROE. And we like to see that management teams continuing to reinvest that capital at those attractive rates.

We like high-profit margins, the higher the better, because it indicates a company is either soundly beating its competition or has barely any competition at all. If a company can maintain a high net profit margin over many years and through economic cycles gives clear numerical proof of its superiority.

We would prefer the first three companies over the last three compa-nies any time.

We have selected three companies with stable and/or rising profit margins with time (Facebook, Mastercard, and Visa) and three other companies with declining profit margins with time (General Electric, Sears, and Schlumberger). What you notice is that ultimately higher earnings drive stock prices higher and vice versa. Always remember the market, in the long run, is a weighing machine, but in the short-term, it is a voting ma-chine. The market always rewards strong growing companies much more than they do poor, underperforming companies that are crumbling.

(1) Examples of Companies with Stable / Rising / Improving Profit Margins and ROE

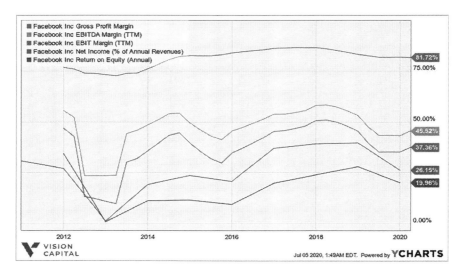

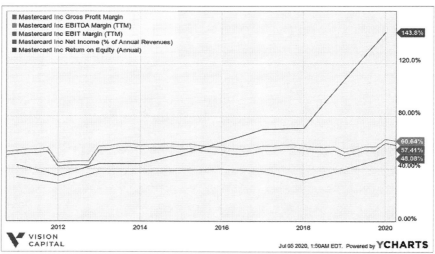

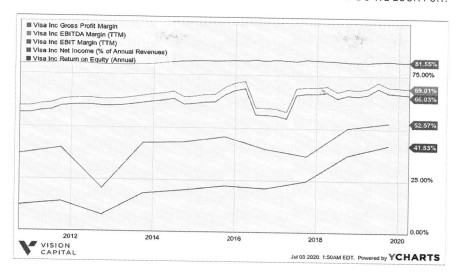

Eventually, Higher Stock Prices Follow Higher Earnings...

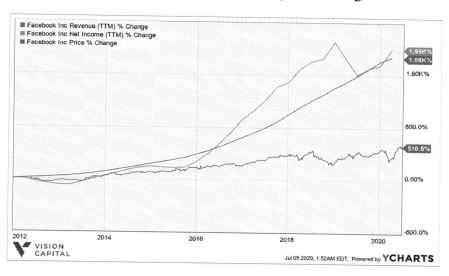

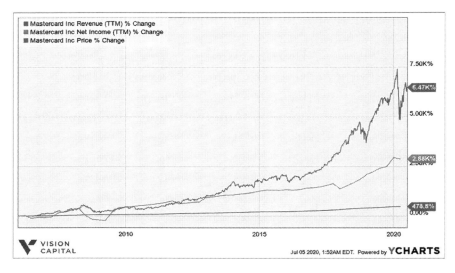

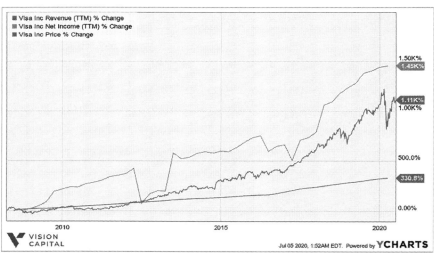

(2) Examples of Companies with Low and/or Declining Profit Margins and ROE

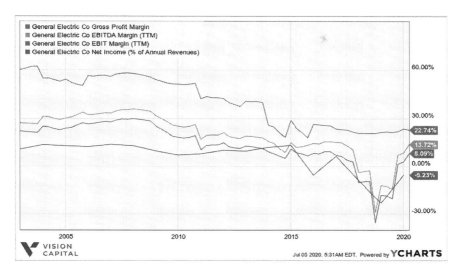

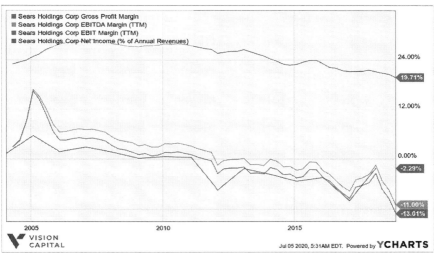

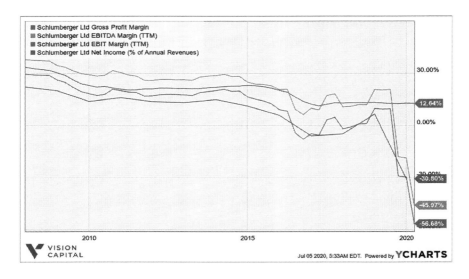

Eventually, Lower Price Follows Lower Earnings...

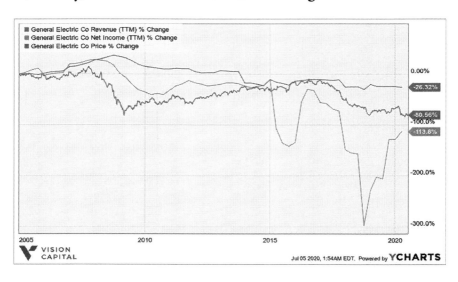

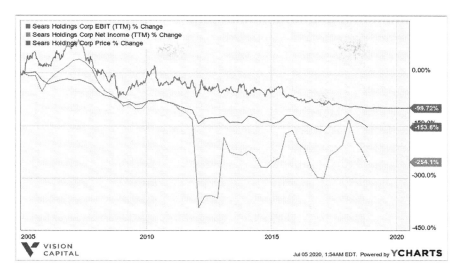

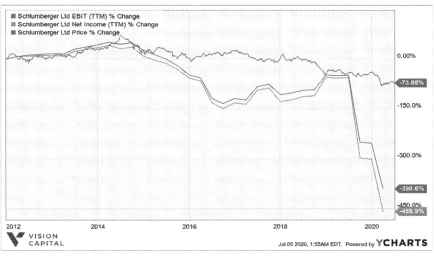

Why the Importance of Capital Allocation Skills?

Great capital allocation does not just happen. Yet every great performing stock that has staying power north of five or ten years has a talented financial team that makes intelligent capital allocation decisions.

Here are some of the questions we would like you to ask:

1) Is the company using excess cash to pay dividends?
2) Does that indicate that it does not have healthy growth prospects, attractive market opportunities, or the best reinvestment opportunities?
3) Or does it indicative awesome discipline, like we typically see for Dividend Aristocrats over the years (a group with tremendous market-beating history that keeps increasing dividends consistently year after year).
4) Is the company buying back its stock?
5) Is it a routine schedule just to offset dilution from stock options? That would be a negative for us.
6) Or does it have a plan to jump in headfirst and buy back shares at discounted prices? In this approach, it stockpiles cash, then buys back huge chunks of stock at the right prices.
7) Is the company making smart acquisitions that build long-term value for shareholders?
8) Does it issue stock for a large acquisition? Studies show two out three of these fail.
9) Does the management team have a long history of successful acquisitions with zero or few write-downs on what it buys?
10) Do the acquisitions enhance the company's competitive edge, or are they part of an empire-building strategy by a CEO simply interested in running a larger business?

Why Do We like Financially Strong Companies with Net Cash, Little or No Debt

How does the company use debt? Excess leverage (aka debt levels) can lead to bankruptcy, fraud, or desperation. **We really like companies with preferably net cash, with little or no debt.** But the smart use of debt is crucial because we never know when the next sudden downturn will come and revenues might come to a sudden standstill. The business would still be able to last through a sudden and temporary economic downturn.

But ultimately **net cash/debt has to be looked at relative to the operating and free cash flow burn** (especially for companies that are not profitable). So, for example, if a company has $600mil of net cash and $10mil of negative free cash flow (but showing a trend of improving FCF) that is probably okay. But if the company has only $30mil of net cash then we would definitely be more concerned and watching it closely.

Ultimately, we are looking for winners who survive and thrive, not **winners who thrive but cannot survive**. Because if the latter cannot even survive a sudden and temporary economic slowdown, they will not be there to ride the up move when the economy eventually recovers.

If the company has significant debt, we look at (1) **current ratio and cash ratios** to determine if current assets or cash is sufficient to cover existing current liabilities and (2) **net interest coverage ratios** to ensure that the company has sufficient cash to cover interest expenses.

Below is just some rough guidance:

No.	Ratio	Formula	Rough Guidance
1	Net Cash[52] (Debt)	**Add:** Cash + ST & LT Investment **Less:** ST & LT Debt	Should be > 3 in ratios compared to OCF and FCF
2	Current Ratio	Current Assets Current Liabilities	Preferably >2, minimum >1. (2=current asset twice of current liabilities)

---

[52] Note most financial literature reports Net Cash as Total Cash minus Total Liabilities. So our definition is different, but what we are interested in is how liquid the company can get, because often working capital (accounts receivables, payables, inventory) is something that is crucial and has to be used to run the business. Thus if the company has sufficient liquidity to pay off all its debt with its cash and investments.

3	Cash Ratio	$\dfrac{\text{Cash + ST \& LT Investments}}{\text{Current Liabilities}}$	Preferably >1, minimum >0.5 (enough cash to pay off current liabilities)
4	Debt/ Equity Ratio	$\dfrac{\text{Debt}}{\text{Equity}}$	Preferably =0, maximum <0.5. Company solvent, unlikely liquidation.

When you read through the numbers that we are looking at (sales growth, return on investments, capital allocation, debt levels on the balance sheet), none of these sound like the quarterly earnings numbers that you will see quoted so much by the so-called "The Wise". A number of their analysis are quite good, but if you are thinking about your investment as a business of which you are a part-owner, you want to think about the long-term trends and inputs of that business, not whether profit margins compressed by 10bps (i.e. 0.10%), revenues, or earnings were missed by a whisker.

Why Do We like Strong past Price Appreciation?

This will be contrary to buying low and selling high, which is what most investors are taught. Many people prefer to buy a stock that has been crushed and to sell it on the rebound when the market warms up to it recovering. They are shopping on the discount rack on the thrift store rather than on Fifth Avenue. Who does not like cheap bargains, either on purchases or stocks?

We prefer to be contrary about how we think. While there is nothing wrong with buying something on sale, **we don't mind buying high**. In fact, **we even seek it out**, because a **high price means that the market has recognized a winning company**. You will find that some of these winners will continue to double, double, and double over the years to become one of our outstanding performers.

Consider an investor's take on Newton's law of inertia: **"A stock on the rise tends to remain on the rise unless an outside force disrupts its path."** The best growth companies continue rising because their advantages allow them to sustain remarkable earnings and cash flow growth and to continuously win new converts among the ranks of both customers and investors. We make sure these companies have all the qualities that we are looking for because when we find excellence, invest in excellence, and hold excellence, these companies can sustain a remarkably higher extended run.

> *"Because **winners win, and they tend to keep winning**.*
> *That is why **we look for winners in the winning pile to invest**,*
> *never losers in the losing pile."*
> *- Eugene Ng*

Grossly Overvalued According to the Financial Media

Finally, one of the **most radical and non-conforming principles** when it comes to Vision Investing, and one of the principles that **make us truly different** from Wall Street and the traditional investors is "**grossly overvalued stocks**".

Being derided as overvalued is a trait that many smart investors avoid but **we like to hear...stocks that go on to double, triple, quintuple, and more over the years**. The "too expensive" label comes from underestimating how one of these companies can disrupt its industry, displace competitors, and grow over a relatively short period. Fear of paying too much may leave many investors on the sidelines, **only to come in later and drive the stock up further** when the writing on the wall becomes more apparent.

We have seen this play out many times before. As a company continues to perform and prove skeptics wrong, the company and the stock will converge as doubters become believers and buy the stock. And as more money comes into the stock, it will go up.

So next time, when you come across a company that has most of our criteria and CNBC or some Bloomberg headline is saying that the company's stock price is so overvalued because its PE is so high, or its stock price has run up too much to make it a good value, we can **almost guarantee you that you are looking at a very good investment**.

Remember, **we are searching for first-rate companies** and many of these companies **will be priced more expensive** than the second-rate or third-rate ones. And it is these first-rate companies that **we are hunting for**.

Overall Financials: What Do We Look For?

1. Growing companies with exceptional business models that generate bountiful earnings or cash flows.
2. High returns on capital and talented management teams that put money to work in even higher return ventures.
3. Strong balance sheets with appropriate levels of cash and debt to take advantage of growth opportunities without sacrificing long term flexibility or being beholden to the capital markets
4. A high but sustainable profit margin, ideally one that's expanding.
5. Strong past appreciation and outperformance.

Overall Financials: How Do We Find What We Are Looking For?

Public companies generally release financial information quarterly. You can find these filings, known as 10-Qs and 10-Ks on a company's investor relations website (you can Google "[Company Name] investor relations) or at SEC.gov. Although these filings highlight different aspects or segments of a company's business, they will all contain three key financial statements:

1) Income statement
2) Balance sheet
3) Cash flow statement.

No.	Financial Statement	What to look out for?
1	Income Statement	**Used:** To calculate sales and profit growth and profit margins. **Like:** Continuously rising sales and rising profit margins. **Implications:** Profits increasing faster than Sales.
2	Balance Sheet	**Used:** To examine a company's capital structure (debt vs equity) and how well it is able to fund future operations. **Like:** Net Cash with little or no debt relative to FCF burn. **Implications:** Understand if the company has ample cash to fund future growth and debt restrictions will not force it to make short-term decisions at the expense of long-term growth.
3	Cash Flow Statement	**Used:** To determine if a company is generating cash as it is growing **Like:** Positive, improving, and growing Operating Cash Flow (OCF) and Free Cash Flow (FCF) from the business. **Implications:** If the business is self-sustaining with positive cash flows and does not need to raise additional cash to fund growth.

Summary Financials Checklist

1. Sales that were higher this year than the last two years
2. A sales growth that was higher this year than last year
3. Profit margin that was higher this year than last year
4. Healthy returns on equity with manageable levels of debt relative to operating earnings
5. A healthy balance of cash and long-term debt
6. Owner earnings growth that can accelerate
7. Strong past appreciation and outperformance

QUICK SUMMARY

- The best-performing stocks tend to be the ones with **high rates of sales growth and eventually rising profits and cashflows**.
- Look for stocks with **rising and improving profit margins,** especially when the business has operating leverage.
- We love financially strong companies with **net cash and little to no debt.**
- Learn about companies **by reviewing them every 3 months** via their quarterly earnings results.

CHAPTER 18

WHY CULTURE & MANAGEMENT AND WHAT DO WE LOOK FOR?

Culture and Management are extremely interlinked and extremely difficult to talk about one without the other. So, though we have each in different sections in our four pillars, we have combined the two to be covered in one chapter. In short, leadership teams matter, culture matters.

Culture & Management: Why Do We Look for It?

Culture reflects all the connections happening for an organization. The culture is how the company interacts and treats all its **stakeholders, its employees, customers, suppliers, and shareholders**. This is one of the most important if not **the greatest determinant of long-term success for any business**. The companies that **focus on treating all their key constituents well tend to thrive over decades**, and that kind of positive culture is far more important than to our focus on being a business-owner investor than quarterly earnings reports and short-term price fluctuations.

Great culture does not just happen overnight. A **tremendous amount of work and effort** goes behind the scenes to set it up for long term success. It is not just about trying to make people happy. **Happy, productive, passionate, and purpose-driven employees** are our ultimate aims.

When it comes to **management, good management trumps almost all other concerns.** Better a mediocre business with great management than a great business with mediocre management. Because it is **only a matter of time that mediocre managers will run a great business to the ground**.

Now imagine **great management in great companies—that is a winning combination**. Yes, it is subjective, but we are equipped with these skills to know. Find a video on the internet of how they interact with the audiences. Are they smart, visionary, and inspiring? You will get a rough sense.

Culture & Management: What Do We Look for?

To many, culture feels vague, difficult to quantify, and is definitely more qualitative and much more an art vs science. **Culture to us starts at the top, with the CEO first.** But when we see a founder CEO, we definitely pay attention. This is especially true when a CEO has stuck with their company through the IPO and past needing money. If they still decide to stick around even after raking millions if not billions from an IPO, there's clearly continued passion for the business they created. That passion will eventually spread to the employees working there.

On and on, you can find these companies, but that's not a guarantee of success. There are many founders who are ego-driven, incompetent, and fraudulent. But overall, if you **find a great company with great culture and a founder who's the CEO**, that should be a very positive sign when fishing in the public markets.

The second data point that we love to understand, and typically it is a tough number to find, is a **company's employee retention rate**. Ideally, **we want a business that is keeping its people, promoting from within, and building a lasting culture that supports employees as key stakeholders**. We want a culture where people are staying because the cost of retraining new employees is expensive and painful. This is especially true for positions steeped in institutional knowledge and key management positions.

Whenever we meet any employee at any company that we are thinking of investing in, we want to hear from them: "**I am grateful to work here. I am proud to work here. I am thankful for my job.**" These are typically strong indicators that the employees are truly loving working in their job.

A great resource you can use is Glassdoor, which publishes an annual "Best Places to Work" list. In addition, **Fortune** publishes "100 Best Companies to Work For." These are excellent resources and a great starting point for you to find companies that are extremely well managed with employees who love working there. **Well-run, happy employees often lead to great companies.**

Culture & Management: How Do We Look for It?

1. **Ownership Structure that is vested and aligned with shareholder's interests.**
   a. Insider ownership and compensation (Form 14A Proxy Statement), typically more than 5% insider ownership preferred or executives who own meaningful personal stakes and executive compensation seems fair relative to the size and performance of the business.
   b. Insider buys and sells (Form 4 SEC Filings)
   c. High quality of directors and board members

2. **Higher Purpose that inspires long-term growth**
   a. Company values and mission statement (Form 10K Annual Report)
   b. Shareholder letter from CEO (if available)
   c. Company website (investor relations)

3. **Evidence that when the business wins, customers, employees, and the world also win.**
   a. Industry reports, customer reviews, forums, etc.
   b. Evidence that customers love the company's product or service

4. **High levels of employee engagement and CEO approval**
   a. Employee-based Glassdoor overall and CEO approval ratings (>80%) as well as the direction of the historical trend,
   b. Workplace that more than 60% of employees will recommend to a friend via Glassdoor.

Employee Reviews: Case Study of 4 Companies

Anytime, we will prefer the first two companies over the latter two.

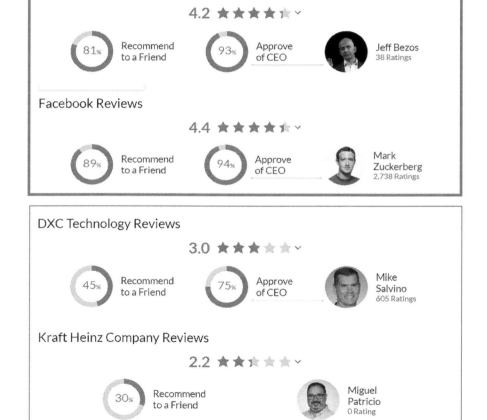

Source: Glassdoor as of June 13, 2020

Summary: Cultural Checklist

A company founder who serves on the board or in company leadership

1. More than 5% insider ownership or executives who own meaningful personal stakes
2. Executive compensation that seems fair relative to the size and performance of the business
3. An employee-based CEO approval rating of more than 80% via Glassdoor
4. A workplace that more than 60% of employees would recommend to a friend via Glassdoor.
5. Evidence that customers love the company's product or service.
6. A clear, transparent purpose that resonates with you.
7. Diversity (race, age, gender) on the board and within management.
8. Ability to hire and retain talented workers

QUICK SUMMARY

- The culture is how the company interacts and treats all its **stakeholders,** its **employees, customers, suppliers, and shareholders**.
- **Mediocre managers** will eventually run a great business to the ground.
- Good **company culture** starts at the top with the CEO.

CHAPTER 19

HOW DO WE THINK DIFFERENTLY ABOUT VALUATIONS?

Be Approximately Right, Not Precisely Wrong

Investors **who do not love spreadsheets and math will love us**. A number of the companies we invest in **can be really difficult to assess by traditional valuation metrics**, like traditional simple price-earnings (PE) ratio or complicated discounted cash flow (DCF) calculations. While all companies are ultimately valued on their ability to produce cash from their operations, we tend to operate in a state of flux that trying to predict their future with any numerical precision is a questionable prospect.

Imagine most sell-side equity research analysts from the banks **cannot even successfully pin down what the company will earn in any given quarter**, even after the sales are all correct. How can one rely on their prediction (i.e. price targets) of how much the same company will sell in one year, out to two decimal places? This problem literally gets worse when the company is rapidly gaining market share, creating new demand, and seeing high digit double growth all subject to volatility. What we are trying to do here is **to be approximately right rather than to be precisely wrong.** It does not mean analysis is unimportant. In fact, it's more important than ever.

PE Ratio: The Market's Price Tag for a Company

One of the most common methods, most people use to evaluate stocks: the **price-to-earnings ratio** (the P/E ratio). P/E equals the price of a stock divided by the company's earnings per share (EPS) over the past twelve months.

$$\text{Price-to-Earnings (PE) Ratio} = \frac{\text{Stock Price}}{\text{Earnings per Share (EPS)}}$$

Not All PEs Are Created Equal

Let's take two examples:

Sucky Bubble Tea Corp (Ticker: SUCK), the retailer of exotically flavored bubble tea, has EPS of $0.50 and a stock price of $5. Thus, its **PE ratio is 10** (i.e. $5 / $0.50).

Windows Incorporated (Ticker: WIN), the software conglomerate whose operating software Windows has suddenly cracked a competing brand's seemingly unshakable hold on the personal computing market, has EPS of $2.00, and trades at $120. Thus, its **PE ratio is 60** (i.e. $120 / $2).

The PE for a given stock varies on changes in **price** (which **happens every day**) and **changes in earnings** (which **happen once a quarter**). This is extremely crucial; we want you to sit on it and think about it for the next minute.

Think of PE ratio as the price tag that the market has in order for you to buy shares in these companies. So, using the above, the market is saying, "If you want to **buy stock in SUCK**, you have to **pay 10 times the company's earnings** and respectively you have to **pay 60 times earnings** to **buy shares in WIN**.

Buying stocks Iike WIN that trades at 35 times earnings of higher (as do many of the growth stocks) is akin to shopping at Tiffany's; you **pay high prices for desired goods**. Purchasers of stocks at 10 times earnings or less have opted to shed their discretionary income on the equity equivalent of a **bargain bin**.

Looking closer at the two examples, you think this is too good a deal to pass up. The absolute price is low at $5 versus $120, and you go all in on SUCK. After all, for the same amount of earnings, you have only had to pay $5 per share compared to others who are paying six times more for WIN. You feel like you bought something undervalued and think you have outsmarted the market. You are convinced that the price of SUCK will race to $30 in no matter of time and you start recommending this to your family and friends.

But before you starting pricing Ferraris and yachts, consider what happened 1 year later. WIN ran up to $240 a share (+100%), while SUCK's management closed its seventy-seven SUCKY Hut of the year, sinking the stock to $1.50 a share (-70%).

What you did not realize is that when you bought it a year ago, **SUCK's revenues had already been stagnating and falling**. Management gave **both revenue and profit warnings**, the share price was already down 50% when you bought it, and revenues and profits fell 30% and 50% respectively. SUCK had **a lot of debt** on the balance sheet and the stores were not managed. There was a **lack of fiscal discipline in-store expansion,** and they **struggled with respect to innovation** in the beverages they sold. A year later, the revenues declined even faster, down 40%, and the SUCK became **unprofitable with negative EPS** of -$1 and bleeding cash rapidly.

Conversely, **WIN grew rapidly, revenues were up +40%, and cash flow and profits expanded faster at +60% and +55% with operating leverage**. The company had a market share of 10% which **doubled** from two years before and **disrupted and gained market share rapidly** against the existing incumbent who had 55% market share and lost market share twice as rapidly compared to WIN. WIN now had **recurring revenues of** more than 95% and **existing customers spent 120% more** than the year before. **New customers were added at +25% growth rates**. The company had **zero debt and had net cash** instead. WIN was run by a **visionary CEO and co-founder** who **owned more than 10%** of the company, and WIN had been named in Fast Company's 100 **most innovative companies** and **Top 50 companies to work** for in the last three years.

The lesson: <u>Not all PE ratios are created equal.</u> Some stocks may be considered underpriced at 55 times earnings, whereas others may be grossly overpriced when their PE rises to 14. The market's price tag is based on past history, present circumstance, and future projections, all of which vary from company to company and industry to industry. **It can be worth paying more for high-quality businesses.** We would rather pay more to buy the best businesses than to pay less for any businesses (including wonderful) at undervalued prices.

> *"It's **far better to buy a wonderful company at a fair price** <u>than</u>*
> *<u>a fair company at a wonderful price</u>."*
> *- Warren Buffett*

Also, it is more important to look at it deeply and follow the framework provided to help guide and allow you **to separate the winners from the losers**. Trust us, there are such companies like WIN; we just have to look hard enough and be different from the crowd.

PE Ratio and Growth Rates

One more thing about growth rates: all else being equal, a 20% grower selling at 20X earnings (i.e. PE of 20X) is a much better buy than a 10% grower selling at 10X earnings (i.e. PE of 10X). What is key to understand is **the earnings of the faster growers really drive the increase in the stock price**.

Look at the widening gap in earnings between a 20% grower and a 10% grower that both start with the same $1.00 in EPS.

Year	Company A 20% EPS Growth EPS $1.00 EPS (A)	Company B 10% EPS Growth EPS $1.00 EPS (B)
0	$1.00	$1.00
1	$1.20	$1.10
2	$1.44	$1.21
3	$1.73	$1.33
4	$2.07	$1.46
5	$2.49	$1.61
6	$2.99	$1.77
7	$3.58	$1.95
8	$4.30	$2.14
9	$5.16	$2.36
10	$6.19	$2.59

In the beginning, Company A is selling for $20 a share (20X earnings of $1 EPS) and by the end of 10 years, it sells for $123.80 (20X earnings of $6.19 EPS). Company B starts out selling for $10 a share (10X earnings of $1 EPS) and ends up selling for $25.90 (10X earnings of $2.59 EPS).

Even if the PE ratio of Company A is reduced from 20X to 15X because investors don't believe it can keep up its fast growth, the stock would still be selling for $92.85 (15X earnings of $6.19 EPS) at the end of 10 years. Either way, **you'd rather own Company A than Company B**.

Note that we did not work for 30% growth rates or higher. That level of growth is very difficult to sustain for three years much less ten years.

This, in a nutshell, is the key to the big baggers and why 20% of growers produce huge gains in the market, especially over a number of years. It is all based on the arithmetic of compounded earnings.

Now to some real-life examples….

A Real-Life Lesson from Amazon

On April 28, 2016, Amazon traded at **PE of 250X** (most financial media called it "grossly overvalued"). Amazon had announced their 1Q16 earnings that very day. Amazon's net sales were up +28%YoY, **free cash flow was +101%YoY, and operating income +320%YoY**. Specifically, AWS net sales were +64%YoY, operating income +210%YoY.

If most investors were to solely focus on Amazon's PE of 250X, they would never invest in Amazon. But when one realizes that earnings and cash flows can grow much faster than sales, the stock price can still go up even higher. Over the next couple of years, one should not be surprised to expect PE to fall, but **EPS grew by +472%,** and the **stock price still went up by +222%**.

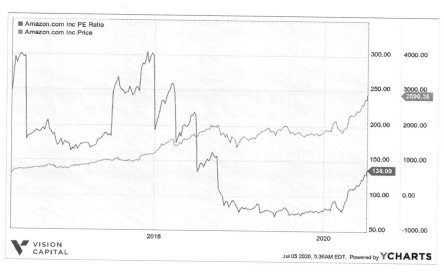

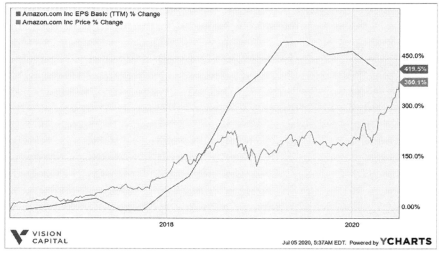

Source: YCharts (April 28, 2016 – July 05, 2020)

High PE businesses can be worth investing if accompanied by strong earnings growth.

Summary

The criteria provided is **not guaranteed to weed out all the losing companies or to point you to every winner.** But they **offer a framework for evaluating fast-growing companies** that can **focus your attention on the characteristics most likely to be shared by companies that turn growth into extraordinary performance over a long period**. Anyone can beat the market. You just need to appreciate, understand, and pay attention to the 4 pillars we have laid out. In Vision Investing, it really is not that complicated.

QUICK SUMMARY

- Some companies **can be really difficult to assess by traditional valuation metrics** like price-earnings (PE) ratio or discounted cash flow (DCF) calculations.
- Not all PEs were created equal.
- When considering **growth rates**, understand **earnings of these fast growers will eventually drive the increase in the stock price.**

CHAPTER 20

HOW DO WE THINK ABOUT RISKS AND WHAT CAN POSSIBLY GO WRONG?

Risk is part of investing in equities and especially in single name stocks like we do. Ultimately, **there are risks to any investment in any business. We must understand them and be prepared for them** when they do happen, so we will know how and what to react.

This chapter really focuses on **what can possibly go wrong**.

It really boils down to three things that we look at:

1. Leadership Succession Planning
2. Threat of Disruption on the Horizon
3. Too Big to Succeed

(1) Leadership Succession Planning

As you have figured out by now, **our style of investing involves putting our capital and our faith in the hands of corporate leaders.** Imagine that they are flying an airplane and you are one of the passengers. Just like in a plane, you have no control in the public markets (so stop thinking you have). How confident are you that your pilot will get you to your destination safe and sound?

That's **why we placed a lot of emphasis on the best corporate leaders**. When you have the best, you can feel confident that pilots like these won't fall asleep at the stick or try something funny. And since you will not and cannot change your pilot mid-flight like you do for your CEO or co-founder, you better like him or her. And when the time comes to hit the fence, you have the full confidence that your CEO will be able to rough it out and deal with it. But also, if your pilot quits, is there a co-pilot to take over? Is the co-pilot ready and the right person to land safely?

Business is the same way, and it **starts with the first transition from the founder to the next leader.** It worked well when Bill Gates handed the Microsoft reins to Satya Nadella or when Tim Cook took over Steve Jobs's position at Apple, but will it always?

When Howard Schultz left Starbucks, the results weren't pretty. When Schultz departed, a large part of Starbucks's culture and success left with him. For five years, Starbucks struggled...until Schultz returned and revitalized the company.

Because we are long-term investors, who might hold stock in a company longer than any one person's tenure as CEO, **succession planning is an extremely important** consideration.

(2) Threat of Disruption on the Horizon

The second thing that we look for is the **threat of disruption**. We focus on the company's platform, looking for potential downward shifts in the underlying business itself, the broader industry trend, or just the world at large.

An example of disruption is the **shift from desktop to mobile**, where more and more people are spending time with their iPhones and Androids and less with clunky desktops and laptops.

Or **the war on cash**, shift from payment via physical cash and checks to electronic payments. Or on **TV cord-cutting**, where families are no longer watching cable TV and shifting to digital streaming on-demand entertainment instead.

Ultimately, when it comes to such shifts, we think about **which companies will benefit and which will be harmed** by such a platform shift. Who is **most suited to take advantage and best positioned to capitalize**?

(3) Too Big to Succeed

There comes the **law of large numbers**. The **bigger a company gets, the harder it must work to grow and outperform the market**. It is harder to steer a larger aircraft carrier than a much smaller tugboat. Think Intel and Cisco in 2000. In a new technological world, they were the biggest companies with the most cash, and they also had the best talent. They had the most evidence of their own awesomeness. They seemed certain to win. And they were the darlings of the stock market. Yet over the next twenty years, this rosy outlook proved otherwise. Those companies have proved to be mediocre investments, **underperforming the S&P 500 since April 2000 before the dot com bubble crash** (see following chart), as other more nimble companies moved ahead and created new industries and new ways of doing things.

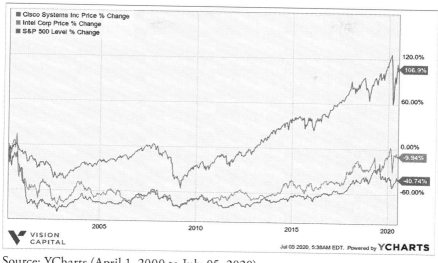

Source: YCharts (April 1, 2000 to July 05, 2020)

We are **also wary of the super-powered winner that everyone loves**. It is possible that sometimes some of our titans and stalwarts might head there and before long, we might stop adding to the stock. It will get too big to succeed.

We find the following chart conveys exactly what we have to say. **As companies keep growing and becoming bigger and bigger, fewer and fewer companies can continue and sustain the fast rates of growth over the long term.** Thus, it is imperative that we seek out these winners and invest and hold them until they start showing signs of a broader decline.

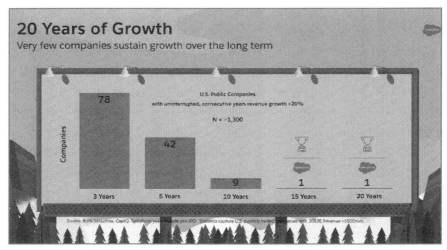

Source: Salesforce.com 2019 Annual Investor Presentation[53]

One of the beautiful things about our markets is that our **markets are constantly refreshed** and **constantly changing. Creative destruction is always happening in every industry and to every company in some way.** There's always something new that is coming up, and that is where we find great long-term opportunities.

Risks & Safety: What Are We Looking for?

1. Evidence that the company is being proactive about disruptive forces or competitors.
2. A talented management bench (plus a leadership succession plan).
3. A company that has still room to grow.
4. Diversification among customers and/or suppliers.

---

[53] Source: Salesforce.com 2019 Annual Investor Presentation https://s23.q4cdn. com/574569502/files/doc_presentations/2019/Dreamforce'19-Investor-Day-Finance-Review-Presentation.PDF

Risks & Safety: How Are We Looking?

Ultimately, the risk factors tend to be **company-specific** with all these factors. We are **looking for tell-tale signs if it is something temporary or a broader longer-term downward spiral**.

You can find most of this in the 10-K and annual reports which typically discusses this, conference calls, or search online for videos of management speaking.

1. Is the company seeing a sudden slowdown in sales growth and revenues?
2. Is the company seeing declining market share? Is the growth in the broader addressable market slowing down? What's the reason?
3. Is the company seeing lower customer retention rates, lower spend, lesser customers being delighted, more negative reviews and press, or a trend of declining NPS scores? What is customer concentration like, is it concentrated in a few customers?
4. Are profit margins being compressed? Is it because of competition? Is the company losing its pricing power?
5. Is the company seeing higher employee turnover, declining Glassdoor ratings of CEO, and fewer employees recommending the company as a good place to work?
6. Is the company reinvesting in itself, devoting adequate resources to R&D? Is there a thriving culture of innovation?
7. Is the company just paying out all of its profits and cash as dividends because it is unable to reinvest their excess cash flows?
8. Is the company going on an acquisition spree and not integrating their acquisitions well enough?
9. Is capable management suddenly resigning and leaving?
10. Does it boil down to more capable competition, or is it just the company's plain inability to execute like before?
11. What are the regulatory risks and risk of competition once the intellectual property protection rights wear off?

12. Is any of the above a temporary one-off or expected to continue for the foreseeable future into a declining phase for the overall business?

Risks & Safety Checklist

- Evidence that the company is anticipating changes in its industry and making plans to address them.
- An array of talented managers who could lead the company if the founder or CEO was no longer involved.
- A consistently rising rate of reinvested cash flows yielding good returns and payback.
- Enough diversity in the customers such that the company does not depend on just a few of them for the majority of its revenue.
- Evidence that the company is aware of regulatory threats and has plans to deal with them.

QUICK SUMMARY

- There are risks when **investing** in any business. The key is to **be prepared.**
- **Reduce risk** by investing in companies with good corporate leaders, a solid plan for disruption, room for growth, and diversity in customers.
- **Evaluate** these companies by reviewing 10-K and **annual reports**, conference calls, or videos of management speaking.

CHAPTER 21

HOW DO WE FIND THESE COMPANIES?

No.	Criteria	Titans of Industry Proven Winners	Emerging Stars Moonshots
1	Sales Growth in the Last Five Years	>5%, >0%	>20%, >15%
2	Gross Profit Margin	>40%	>20%
3	Operating Profit Margin	>10%	Any
4	Net Income Margin	>5%	Any
5	EPS Growth Over Past 5 Years	Positive >0	Any
6	ROE and ROA	>20%, >10%	Any
7	Stock Price Appreciation	Yes	Yes

We will share with you a sample stock screener that you can use to find some of these companies. So for example, based on Finviz, there are currently 7,714 listed companies available. But we **need to really focus on the best.**

Finviz: https://finviz.com/screener.ashx

Below is one example for your review. There are really **no hard and fast rules**, you adjust the criteria and see what you can find. We ignore bio-technology and oil and gas types of companies and see what comes out.

(1) Finding Titans of Industry & Proven Winners
Examples of companies with:
  (a) Sales growth >5%
  (b) Strong profit margins
  (c) Strong returns on capital
  (d) Price appreciation above the last year

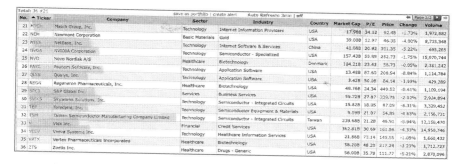

(2) Finding Proven Winners and Emerging Stars
Examples of companies with:
   (a) Faster sales growth >15%
   (b) Even stronger profit margins
   (c) Strong returns on capital
   (d) Positive EPS growth over the last 5 years

(3) Finding Emerging Stars and Moonshots
Examples of companies with:
   (a) Even faster sales growth >30%
   (b) Strong gross profit margins > 50%
   (c) Not yet profitable and negative EPS growth

Source: https://finviz.com/screener.ashx (as of 30 March 2020)

My Favorite Resource: The Motley Fool[54] (https://www.fool.com)

Founded in 1993 by brothers Tom and David Gardner, The Motley Fool helps millions of people attain financial freedom through paid stock recommendation services.

Stock Advisor and **Rule Breakers** are their starter services. I would suggest you look at these first. The Motley Fool has played a large part in how I invest, and I hope it does for you too.

Another informal way to **utilize the Snap Test** covered earlier in Chapter 8, is to find such companies. Basically, these are companies **whose products and/or services matter to us a lot**, and **we don't want them to disappear.**

Go through the exercise on the following pages and hopefully you will find something that might cause you to find out and study more about such companies.

---

[54] PS: This is a not a paid recommendation, and I do not get any compensation from The Motley Fool. This is what has been working for me. I encourage you to go discover and find what works for you.

Exercise: Building your own list of companies that pass your Snap Test

1) **First Column:** Write down 10 **products and/or services** that you **use every day** that you **absolutely love and cannot live without**.
2) **Second Column:** Write the **name of the company** (parent) that owns it.
3) **Third Column:** Is the company **publicly listed** on any stock exchange?

If the company is listed, take a deeper dive into the company.

A sample of mine is listed for example on the following page.

My Sample Exercise
Hope you get the drift by now...

No.	Product or Service	Parent Company	Publicly Listed (Yes/No)
1	Apple iPhone, iPad and Pencil, Airpods, Airpods Pro, Macbook, Safari, ApplePay, AppleTV	Apple	Yes
2	Internet Explorer, Microsoft Word, Excel, Powerpoint, Linkedin, Skype for Business, Teams, One Drive, OneNote, Windows	Microsoft	Yes
3	Google Search, Chrome, Gmail, Google Maps, Google Sheets, Docs, Drive, Translate, Youtube	Alphabet	Yes

What is Your Top 10?

No.	Product or Service	Parent Company	Publicly Listed (Yes/No)
1			
2			
3			
4			
5			
6			
7			
8			
9			
10			

QUICK SUMMARY

- If you want to do it yourself ("DIY"), you can use the free stock screener, **Finviz**, apply the various filters, and add companies to your shortlist. Subsequently, use the framework we had provided to analyze the company further.
- If you would like regular stock recommendations and are willing to pay for it, you can consider paid investing services like The Motley Fool.

PART III
THE LONG-TERM VIEW & MINDSET

WHAT IS THE INVESTOR'S MINDSET YOU NEED TO HAVE?

So far, what we have been doing is weighing the probabilities of investing in your favor by focusing on the following two things:

> (1) **Increasing <u>the probability</u> of success** (finding winners)

> (2) **Increasing <u>the payoff</u> for your winners** (finding multibaggers)

To successfully beat and outperform the market over the long term, you really need to do and have these two things:

1. **Find and invest in companies that will outperform the market**
2. **Have the right investor's mindset and psychology**

We **need you to read this section twice, if not thrice or even ten times**. Because the following chapter is focused on the second part of what is required: the **right investor's mindset and psychology**.

*"The beauty of investing is that **1,000 investors can be in the same great stock company and their returns will be dramatically different**.*

***Finding a great company** is not even half the battle. **Price matters. Time frame matters. Temperament matters. Conviction matters.**"*
- Ian Cassel.

The **biggest obstacle** that often prevents most investors from beating the market is in **our minds, beliefs, mindset, and our psychology**. How we react when we are losing, winning, or when we hear or read something from somewhere (TV, someone, headlines, etc.) is extremely difficult to change almost immediately, though surely, we are of the belief that it can be changed for the better over time.

*"**You are today** where **your thoughts have brought you; you will be tomorrow where your thoughts take you.**"*
- James Lane Allen

We are not telling you what you need to have—for example, **patience, discipline, determination**, etc. because it is **really easy to say, but difficult to internalize** and to apply to ourselves immediately.

Instead, we would rather provide you with the **strategy via a list of winning principles** that are **set for you to follow no matter what happens**. Eventually, that will allow you to appreciate and understand that over time, and it eventually gets built into your own inner system for the better with respect to how you think, feel, and react.

You can find the best companies to go up 5X in the next 10 years, but **if your beliefs and mindset are not wired correctly** when it comes to the first market selloff of 20%, you panic and end up selling everything and not buying some more. You end up missing the entire eventual move higher and never get invested in them.

That is why this section is the most important in the entire book. You can do everything else right, but **if you get this wrong, you have effectively set yourself up for failure from day one.**

"You can have the best fishing rod given to you,
but if you don't know how to use it in the best way possible for you,
it is of no use. You want to master how to use it."
- Eugene Ng

"The greatest mistakes investors make are not logical but psychological.
They neglect simple analytical disciplines that would
protect themselves from their emotions"
- Andy Redleaf

"80% of how you perform when it comes to investing will be
due to your emotions and psychology and
how you react to the market.
Understanding this is the first step to winning."
- Eugene Ng

"To beat the market, we truly need to do something different from the crowd.
We need to be different."
- Eugene Ng

Winning Principles of Vision Investing

1) Own at least 25 stocks.
2) Hold your stocks for a minimum of 5-10 years.
3) Know that 20% of your winners will likely drive 80% of your overall returns.
4) 40% of your stocks will likely lose to the market or lose money.
5) Stocks prices will move 10-40% in any given year.

Winning Principles of Vision Investing

1) **Own at least 25 stocks.**

   a) **Diversification keeps us in the game**, not out of the game.

   b) **Diversification allows us to own multibagger winners**, and we never know which one will be our winners or losers. Let the market prove it to you.

   c) We **take full responsibility for all of our investments. We always do our own due diligence** and **make our own decisions based only on facts,** never emotions.

   d) We follow our investment checklist to **find, invest, and own the best companies that are shaping and making the world a better place.**

   e) **We especially love visionary founder-led and owned companies** that are highly **scalable,** have **large and growing addressable markets, high revenue growth rates, strong competitive advantages, strong and/or improving profit margins** with **operating leverage; growing profits, cash flows,** and **net cash; and little to no debt.**

   f) **All of our companies pass the "SNAP" test,** and we can see them being around for the next 5 years at least and even longer.

2. **Hold our stocks for a minimum of 5-10 years.**

   a) **Stocks go up over the very long term.** Markets **go up 2 out of every 3 years.**

   b) **The longer our investment horizon, the higher the probability of positive returns.** We invest for more than 10 years because it will be 100%.

   c) We are **investors only for the long-term,** that is the only term that counts for us. We know in the short-term, the market is a voting machine (just noise) and in the **long** term, the market is a weighing machine (rewards the best companies).

d) **Find excellence, buy excellence, add to excellence, and sell mediocrity.** That's how we invest. Because **winners always win** and continue to win. Let your winners run high. That is why we always **add to our winners and hold for decades**, not days.

e) We **only invest within our circle of competence.** We clearly know which businesses we want to own and which ones we will not invest in. We only invest in businesses we understand, and we avoid those we do not.

f) We know that **most of the time** when it comes to investing, we **just have to have patience and do nothing.**

3. **Know that less than 20% of our winners will likely drive more than 80% of our overall returns.**

   a) **Unlimited upside, max 100% downside.** We understand that the **maximum stocks can go down is 100%**, but the **maximum stocks can go up is unlimited.**

   b) **4% of all public companies (1 in 25)** have **accounted for close to 100% of all the returns over the past 100 years.** We know that not all of our companies will be winners. But we want to find and invest in these future winners. **We invest in quality, never mediocrity.**

   c) **A few multibagger winners will drive the majority of our portfolio returns and outperformance.** We never trim our winners and sell them. We cannot wait to have our first and many more spiffy-pops[55] to come.

   d) **Our winners over the long run will become more significant**, and our losers become smaller, insignificant, and irrelevant.

   e) The **gains from our winners will far offset all the losses from all our losers.**

---

[55] **Spiffy-Pop:** Imagine a stock climbing more in a single day than your entire cost basis in that position. That's what we call a "spiffy-pop" when that happens.

f) **We always add up on our winners** and water our flowers.

g) **We never double down on our losers** and never water our weeds.

4) **40% of our stocks will likely lose to the market or lose money.**

   a) It is **okay to be wrong,** and **we know we will be wrong from time to time.** But we understand that we need to be wrong in order to be right.

   b) **We always aim to be approximately right** rather than to be precisely wrong.

   c) **We will probably be 50-60% right** and that is okay (if higher, even better).

   d) We **only sell our stocks** when it **no longer follows our original investment thesis** and the business is starting to move towards a **long-term structural decline** and losing its competitive advantage.

5) **Stocks prices will move 10 - 40% in any given year.**

   a) We understand that **markets are always volatile.** We don't know when they might go down, but we know there will **always be market corrections.**

   b) We **relish in volatility** and know that **any of our stock investments will routinely rise or fall 30%-50%+.**

   c) **Stocks will fall faster than they go up in the short-term,** but stocks will eventually rise more than they go down over the long-term.

   d) We know markets typically go **down once every 3 years.**

   e) **We know how often markets fall and by how much:**
      i) **10%** every **year**
      ii) **20%** every **3-4 years**
      iii) **30%** every **10 years**
      iv) **40-50%** every **20-30 years.**

   f) We **relish in volatility** and know that **any of our stock investments will routinely rise or fall 30%-50%+.**

g) **We embrace volatility and market sell-offs and see and use them as bargains and opportunities to add, never to sell.** We are especially greedy when others are fearful.

h) We **keep between 5-20% of our portfolio in cash** to **take advantage of buying opportunities** to **add to our highest convictions** during such market declines. While cash is a drag on returns during bull markets, it provides stability during stock market volatility, helps us **keep a cool head** during periods of panic and **gives us ammunition** to take advantage of bargain prices.

It's true that many fortunes are made and lost during times of excessive pessimism in the markets. Having the proper mindset doesn't prevent you from feeling despair when the market drops. We aren't robots, after all.

But **having the right mindset** does give you the **tools to overcome your own worry and fear** and to **act decisively when opportunities arise.** You can see the fear, feel the fear, and have the confidence to profit from it.

Yes, those days are coming, and none of us knows when.

Recognize that **volatility is the price of admission** in order to **participate in the stock market's powerful long-term performance**. That's especially true when we're dealing with dynamic, fast-growing companies, which often trade at a premium price relative to their current earnings power. These companies carry a burden of lofty expectations, which means that any missteps will be magnified, and the short-term sell-offs can be severe. By investing in companies, we believe in strongly and **focusing our sights firmly on the future**, we can **endure the inevitable downturns** and **let the power of long-term compounding work on our behalf**.

It's clichéd to say that fate favors the prepared mind, but it's true. It's also incomplete. For when you get right to it, **fate actually favors the prepared psyche**. More than anything, we want you to be in the best position to win in the markets. And our checklist principles will help you get there.

What Investing Requires You to Have:

(1) Patience & Discipline

Patience is by far the most important financial skill in investing.

> *"**Money doesn't grow overnight**. No matter how great the talent or efforts,*
> *some things just take time. You can't produce a baby in*
> *one month by getting nine women pregnant."*
> *- Warren Buffett*

Malcolm Gladwell's book *Outliers* looks at a number of "outliers," people who are extraordinarily proficient in certain subjects or skills. It then tries to break down what helped them become outliers. According to Gladwell, one common factor among these carefully selected individuals was the amount of time they practiced within their area of study. It appeared that only by reaching 10,000 hours of practice (that's about 90 minutes per day for 20 years) could one become an outlier. To use another of Gladwell's popular terms, 10,000 hours is the "Tipping-Point" of greatness. **Know that you will need commitment and time to master something; mastery does not come overnight.**

(2) Discipline via Commitment and Consistency

When you slow down, set goals, and concentrate on consistent performance, you will usually deliver exactly what you say you will. In other words, "slow and steady wins" is aspirational, a statement acknowledging the power of consistency.

When it comes to investing, the slow and steady will win the race eventually. We are at our best when we slow down, set goals, and concentrate on consistent performance. We usually deliver exactly what we say we will. It is really the power of consistency.

The **goal is not to be perfect**, but **instead to have progress**. Understand that investing **often feels like three steps forward** and **one step backward**.

Focus on the bigger picture, the eventual progress, the **net two-step steps forward**, not the one step backward.

Investing is a marathon, not a sprint. **In the short-term, it is just noise.** You shouldn't fixate on short-term underperformance given how random the market can behave over shorter time frames. However, it's perhaps just as important to remember that this randomness works both ways, and you should never let short-term outperformance motivate you to completely abandon your process in hopes of repeating that outperformance.

(3) Invest in Companies You Understand

Know your circle of competence. What you know, what you don't know. Invest in companies that you can understand, if you don't, then do not. A litmus test in addition to the Snap Test, is we ask ourselves if the company can grow bigger in the next 5 years, if not, we don't invest.

> *"Don't invest in a company whose business you don't understand."*
> *- Warren Buffett*

For us, that's the reason we do not invest in oil, commodity and shipping companies, banks, biotech, or pharmaceutical companies for example. What are the types of companies you will not invest in?

(4) Think like an Owner

Thinking like an owner changes your whole perspective on stock investing. Likewise, you should have the same perspective with stocks. When you are buying a stock, you are owning the company, not buying ticker symbols.

> *"If you are going to **own a new car**, you will*
> *think about its **fair valuation**,*
> *you will think about its **features** and you will **compare** it with cars*
> *offered by other manufacturers from the same segment.*
> *Then **after checking everything, you will decide which one to buy**."*
> *- Warren Buffett*

(5) Find Great Companies & Invest for the Long Run

Do not try to predict **how a stock will do**. On any given day, the odds of winning are probably similar to that of a coin toss with about a 50/50 chance.

Focus instead on thinking in the long-term of how a business will do. Rather than trading in the short term, a far better strategy is to simply **identify great businesses and hold them as long as their competitive advantages remain intact. Don't find great valuations. Find great businesses.**

Because **valuations are temporary. Good businesses are not**. Don't buy on dips for your starter positions. **Great businesses tend to dip only almost briefly**. They always end up sizzling and going higher. You insist on buying on dips, you will probably miss the entire move higher and never end up investing in them. Take an initial small starter position first. You can always add more later.

(6) Buy When Everyone is Selling

Keep calm, stay focused on the long term, and take advantage of bargain opportunities.

"Be fearful when others are greedy, and
greedy when others are fearful."
- Warren Buffett

(7) Trust Yourself to Be a Successful Investor

To be successful, you need to overcome the fear and not pay attention to what others are telling you. Accumulate understanding and create investment choices to stand apart from the crown and be a winner on your own

"The hardest thing is to trust your investment decisions.
You always think that others are right and you are wrong.
Instead, you need to study and believe in yourself.
I always knew I was going to be rich. I don't think I doubted for a minute"
- Warren Buffett

(9) Realize the Complexity of Past Successes. Never Be Overconfident.

We think this is especially true in investing, where during one bull market, you do really well, and therefore assume, "Here's what I did during this bull market, and therefore, I will do it again. I will take what I did last time and do it again," without realizing that markets evolve over time and what worked during one period of time might not work during the next period of time.

Especially if you end up **having more confidence or overconfidence** with your investing abilities, it will **eventually lead to poor returns.**

(10) Understand Bad Days Are Inevitable.

Getting sick, sleeping too little, poor weather, getting injured, travel plans gone awry; no matter how much you train and plan in advance, the chance that every race in your career goes off without a hitch probably rounds to 0%.

Likewise, **we don't know of a single investor who has a perfect record of investing in market-beating stocks—no such investor exists** (so stop chasing to be one!). Fortunately, investing in a stock that goes on to perform poorly doesn't guarantee a poor career. What's important is that you don't get hung up on suboptimal outcomes. Instead, **seek to learn from what went wrong**. Mistakes can make for learning experiences that set you up for future success if you let them.

(11) There Will Be a Lot of Days When the Market Will Fall

There will be days where the market will fall and **trust us, there will be a lot of these**. And when it happens, you can feel emotional and isolated or even feel that it is not working. But that's the cost of investing. And ultimately, we're going to be OK with that, because we know there are more days when the market goes up. We're in this together. **Look at your portfolio at most once a day, never more frequent than that.** In fact, we tend to **do it only after the market closes** because it prevents us from having itchy fingers to want or try to do something (buy or sell something) that we are sure you will most likely regret not long after.

If you need a break, take one. If that means ignoring the news, or not looking at TV (CNBC, Bloomberg), Facebook, Twitter, do what you need to do to clear your head. When you're ready, come back. Personally, we go exercising, go for a walk, a run, go to the beach, go hiking, enjoy the sun, the greenery, the sunset or the birds, nature, or just spend time with your loved ones and family. There are more things to life than investing.

(12) Investing Is Boring, Not for Excitement

If you want excitement, go do something else. Go to the casino (not that we are advocating), skydiving, or just do something else with your life. But don't do it with your investments and your money. Instead, why not try to learn a new language or skill, read a book, watch a movie or drama on Netflix?

(13) Every Investor Should Have an End Goal in Mind

Be it saving for retirement, leaving money to family members, or buying a dream home, that is your **end goal**—your 42km marathon finishing line.

It's **critical for you to both develop a plan for getting you across that finish line and to stick to it**. Get caught up chasing short-term gains, and you may find yourself hitting the investing equivalent of the runner's wall.

QUICK SUMMARY

- The **biggest obstacle** that often prevents most investors from beating the market is in **our minds, beliefs, mindset, and our psychology.**
- Patience is by far the most **important financial skill** in investing.
- Adopt the winning principles of **Vision Investing.**
- The goal with investing is **not to be perfect**, but **instead to make progress**.

CHAPTER 23

WHEN DO WE EVER SELL?

Knowing when to sell is a crucial yet overlooked aspect of investing. Snagging shares at a bargain can mean absolutely nothing if you don't sell when you should. Sadly, we can't give you "The Laws of Selling." We heartily agree with Philip Fisher who said, "If the job has been correctly done when a common stock is purchased, **the time to sell it is — almost never.**"

Selling is not something we talk a lot about. For one, **we prefer buying and holding excellent companies rather than trading stocks**. And second, studies have shown that **individual investors harm their returns by trading too much**, trying to time buy and sell points.

Yet we also know that there are times when you want to or need to sell some positions. And there are times when we want you to sell positions.

For the most part, we don't think that we should ever sell, but there are circumstances where it makes sense. Most of the time, it really ultimately belongs to either of the **two categories**:

1) Specific to **You (6 Rules #1-6)**
2) Specific to the **Stock (11 Rules #1-11)**

These are our reasons to sell stocks, ranked in order.

6 Rules to Sell Stocks (You - Specific Reasons)

Rule #1: Don't Sell

Our first rule of selling is, "Don't sell." The historical data from rising stock markets inside an expanding universe proves that to optimize our lifelong returns, **we should hold forever.** If that sounds absurd, refer to the Buffett quote above. In our principles, **"forever" starts with a mandated five-year investment. Our best returns will come from stocks we hold for 10-20 years at least.** Along the way, we'll endure some egregious declines and wish we'd bailed. And **not every stock will be a big winner; in fact, most will not matter much in the end.** What we definitely don't want to do though, is to **sell any of our 50-to-100+ baggers too soon.** Our 5-10 most monstrous long-term winners — unimpeded by tax, transaction, and emotional costs — will make all the difference.

Rule #2: Sell if You're Overbalanced in Equities

One time to **sell is if you're over-allocated toward the stock market relative to your financial profile** (e.g. debt, property, your business, or other financial assets in your overall wealth). For example, if you have unpaid credit card debt at interest rates above 10%, you should sell stocks to pay that off. Finally, if you are so invested that **you will lose sleep or have an emotional breakdown** if your portfolio **loses more than 30%** of its value, then you probably have too much money in stocks and might need to pare down your overall allocation.

Rule #3: Sell if You Have a Limited Time Horizon

The rule of thumb is to **have no money in stocks that we'll need within three to five years.** Going back to 1920, on five separate occasions, the stock market has fallen 35% over a five-year period. Take 1936 – 1941; the Dow Jones Industrials fell nearly 50%. Since it has happened before, it must be possible and will be possible going forward. Who knows when it might happen next? **We simply don't want to be forced to sell stocks when the price isn't right.** And the time to sell stocks will definitely not be after a market decline of 50%!

261

Rule #4: Sell If a Single Position is Too Large

When any holding in our portfolio accounts for more than 20% of our net worth, we can consider gently paring back that position. That percentage ultimately depends on you, for some it could be 5%, others 10% or 20%. The key is to do what works best for you.

That **does depend on a few factors**. For example, if you plan to add significant savings year after year, then a position that large is no problem (so long as you adequately diversify away from it over time). The same holds true if you are early in life and want to concentrate a smaller nest egg on a few bets. But the closer you are to retirement, and the less fresh savings you'll have relative to the existing value of your portfolio, the more resistant you should be to having any stock account for over 20% of your net worth.

We typically don't advocate rebalancing our portfolio (sell our winners and add to our laggards). We believe winners tend to keep winning over time, and we like to let them run. But if a certain position is too big for your comfort, you may want to sell at least some shares.

Rule #5: Sell to Use Money in Your Life

Here again, it's almost absurd to place this rule toward the bottom of the list. **We invest to live a better life, not merely to make money**. But consumer financial data shows that humanity buys far more than it needs, more than it can afford, and more than it will ever optimally use. I'm thankful that my mother taught my brother and me very early to be thrifty and save money, but also to spend our money on learning, experiences, and other people. When you see opportunities to sell stocks to fund those, we say go for it. Otherwise, ask yourself if it's really worth it.

Rule #6: Sell to Give Money to Others

This rule sits at the bottom because we actually think the better move is to gift stocks to charities or to whoever you want. So we suggest gifting, not selling, stock.

12 Rules to Sell Stocks (Stock Specific Reasons)

The four main themes are (1) business change, (2) faulty investment thesis, (3) better opportunities, and (4) it keeps us up at night.

Rules 1-9 largely revolve around business change. There's no way around it: Businesses change — sometimes significantly.

We could be talking about a major acquisition, a change in management, or a shift in the competitive landscape. When this occurs, we **incorporate the new information and reevaluate** to see if the **reasons we bought the company in the first place still hold true**.

We will consider selling if:

- The company's ability to generate profits is affected or clearly struggling.
- Management undergoes significant changes or makes questionable decisions.
- A new competitive threat emerges or competitors perform better than expected.

We'll also take into account **unfavorable developments in a company's industry**. Here, it's **important to understand if this is temporary or permanent**. In a downturn, financial figures may suffer even for the best-run companies. What's important is how these businesses take advantage of the effects on their industry to improve their competitive position.

Rule #1: Sell Small Potatoes

Consider selling stocks whose **value has declined to a minuscule percentage of your portfolio — say, 1% or less**. These tiny positions will have a **negligible impact** on your net worth, **even if they double in value**. It's simply not worth the effort to monitor them. You're better off redeploying that capital into your favorite ideas.

Rule #2: Sell Too Big to Fail

On a related note, **consider selling stocks that have grown to represent an outsize portion of your portfolio** (>10-20%). The answer to "how big is too big" will vary for each investor — some might be comfortable with a single stock accounting for 20% or more or their net worth, while others might prefer that number to be no higher than 5%. The key is to do what works best for you. If you find that one company is causing you to worry excessively or lose sleep, it might be time to pare down that position and diversify your risk.

We don't typically advocate rebalancing your portfolio — selling shares of your best-performing positions and adding to your laggards. We believe that winners tend to keep winning over time, and we like to let them run. But if a certain position is too big for your comfort, you may want to sell at least some shares.

Also, when **companies become too big and approach the law of large numbers, growth starts declining rapidly**. It just **becomes mathematically more challenging** (not that it is not possible) at such rapid growth rates that they are used to in the past. It is far easier for a smaller company to grow 20% at $100mil in revenues and a bigger company with $100bn in revenues. And if a company is indeed not innovating or not expanding their addressable markets and there are **signs of a longer broader structural decline, then you are better off selling**. We usually watch for (1) **slowing or declining TAM growth**, (2) **declining market share vs competitors** and (3) **rapidly declining revenue growth rates that last more than just 1-2 quarters**.

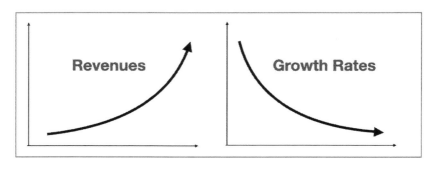

Rule #3: Sell Bad Balance Sheets

When used prudently, debt can help a company accelerate growth and increase profitability. But **leverage is a double-edged sword**. Lenders must be repaid on schedule, even when times get tough. The stress of making debt payments and meeting covenant requirements can cause companies to adopt a short-term mindset or even go out of business altogether.

In contrast, companies with clean balance sheets have flexibility. They can act aggressively when times are tough to capture market share and maybe even acquire distressed competitors.

The **interest coverage ratio** measures how easily a company's earnings can cover its interest payments. It's typically calculated by dividing a company's operating income (earnings before interest and taxes) by its interest payments due during the period. A higher ratio is better, and **anything below 2 is potentially worrisome**.

For those reasons, **we prefer to invest in companies with no or low debt**. But just because a company carries debt doesn't make it an automatic sell candidate. The **key** is to make sure that it is **capable of meeting its debt obligations**. Look for **stable, predictable cash flow** and principal payments spread out years into the future (you can find a company's debt maturity schedule in its annual report). You'll also want to make sure it has a healthy interest coverage ratio, as well as a low ratio of debt to equity. If you **have concerns about a company's debt burden, you may want to sell**.

Rule #4: Sell Fragile Companies

Fragile companies are inflexible, which makes them vulnerable to unexpected developments. They **cannot cope with changing competitive conditions** created by new technology, a natural disaster, or a global pandemic. We want to invest in the companies that can adapt and gain market share in the new environment — and we want to avoid inflexible share donors.

A heavy debt load can make a company fragile. So, can a business model that depends on a single point of failure. Think of a company that relies on a few key customers or a sole-source supplier for a critical input. And beware of companies in cyclical industries or those with low visibility into future revenue. It's tough for such companies to plan expenses and capital projects.

Rule #5: Sell If a Platform Shift Threatens an Investment

Among the **most dangerous threats to any single holding** in our portfolio is a **platform shift away from it**. The transition from horse-drawn carriages to automobiles. From pagers to mobile telephones. From newspapers to the Internet. **Foundational shifts underneath a business that we own can wreak havoc on long-term returns**. The **good news is that these shifts rarely happen overnight**. There's usually too large of an installed base of investors and too much supporting conventional wisdom for there to be a sudden collapse. Change may happen fast, but institutional investors react slowly. **Always keep your eyes open to disruption.**

Rule #6: Sell Shrinking Moats

We love to invest in companies with wide economic moats — a series of advantages that enable them to generate above-average returns on invested capital. But **competition never sleeps and no moat lasts forever**. You might consider selling a company if you **sense that its competitive advantages are starting to shrink**.

Think of consumer-packaged goods giants like Procter & Gamble (NYSE: PG) and Unilever (NYSE: UL). For years, these companies used massive marketing budgets and distribution muscle to capture premium space in consumers' minds and on retailers' shelves. But TV commercials don't have the same impact that they once did, and the internet has made it possible for small brands to build direct relationships with customers. That's caused growth to slow for both P&G and Unilever and forced the companies to slash expenses and invest more in innovation. These are still strong companies with a portfolio of billion-dollar brands, but investors must question whether they deserve a premium multiple — or a spot in their portfolios.

Rule #7: Sell Mediocrity

A **market downturn** can provide the **opportunity to upgrade your portfolio.** This is the **time to sell mediocrity and buy excellence.** If you own second-tier companies, consider upgrading to top dogs. This is your opportunity to upgrade from good to great.

Rule #8: Sell Weak Leadership

Over the last 25 years, the **performance of owner-operated public companies has outperformed the S&P 500 by a multiple of three.** That's **why we like to find CEOs, executives, and board directors that act like owners.** We **love to partner with talented and trustworthy leaders** who have an **inspiring long-term vision and a hefty share ownership stake.** We like CEOs who under promise and overdeliver, who accept criticism, share praises, and produce results, not excuses. This perspective has delivered some of the greatest winners. If the management team at one of your portfolio companies fails to meet these criteria, their stock might be a good sell candidate.

Unfortunately, it stands to reason, then, when a great CEO steps down, the company is more likely to underperform. During Andy Grove's 11-year tenure as CEO of Intel (NASDAQ: INTC), the stock rose 17 times in value, delivering an annualized return of 29%. **Since he stepped down in 1998, the stock has delivered paltry returns.** Succession from a great leader is a very complex transition in the public markets. Keep your eyes open here, too.

Rule #9: Sell If the Company Can't Hold Your Attention

This one may be particular to us, but we are just not interested in owning companies that don't **teach and make us more interested in the world.** These would include businesses that we don't really understand, companies we don't believe in, and organizations that just aren't remarkable. **There are enough great companies out there to fill up our life** with filings and research, news articles, interviews, books, and a lot of thinking. Why buy something that makes us feel like we are in a tired classroom in the primary school?

Rule #10: Faulty Investment Thesis

Everyone makes mistakes. Sometimes, you'll just plain miss something. You should seriously consider selling **if it turns out your rationale for buying the stock was flawed**, if your **original investment thesis was too optimistic**, or if you **underestimated the risks**.

Rule #11: Sell If You've Found a Better Investment

Since these rules are ranked in order, why isn't this one rated higher? Shouldn't we always replace what we have with anything we like more? Probably not. The **data suggests that investors get impatient with an existing holding too often**. They exchange it for the hot stock of today. They hop from dream to fantasy, paying taxes, commissions, and spreads. They never hold long enough to learn about and profit from true greatness.

We **don't oppose buying something we believe in by selling something we don't**. We just **recommend being methodical and intentional about that**. We will not be surprised if, at the end of our investing career, the data shows we would have done better had we never sold a stock. Perhaps the same will be true for you, as well.

Sometimes there's nothing wrong at all with a company or its stock, there are simply better opportunities that bring more bang for your buck.

You can consider selling a less attractive stock (even at a loss) if you think you can get a better deal elsewhere.

Rule #12: Sell Worry Inducers

Do you find yourself obsessing over the operations of a single company? Is there a **particular position that often occupies your thoughts or impacts your sleep**? If so, you should consider following the old adage to "sell to the sleeping point." In other words, reduce your stake so you can sleep and think comfortably once again. Successful investing requires you to think clearly and keep your emotions in check. If you can't stop thinking about a stock, your ability to make quality decisions could be impaired.

Concluding Words...

We **seek to find and invest in businesses** that **continue to grow revenues and profits, have strong balance sheets, sustainable competitive advantages, talented and trustworthy leadership, and pricing power.** Such businesses tend to perform well in times both good and bad, helping investors to beat the market and sleep well at night. If there are companies in your portfolio that don't fit the criteria above, consider selling them and upgrading to stocks that do.

How To Use This Advice

Before we go, we offer you these last suggestions:

1) **Do not feel the need to buy or sell entirely at once.** Eliminate the emotion of investing by incrementally buying and selling.

2) **Add to your winners; subtract from your losers.** Be inclined to part ways with the things you don't believe in, not the things you do. Buy excellence, sell mediocrity.

3) **See the real consequences of selling.** These include taxes, transaction costs, spreads, and mistake-making. They also mean you have to spend time worrying from quarter to quarter what to do next with the money.

4) **Never sell entirely.** If you love learning, why ever sell a position entirely? Don't hide from a mistake or let go of the glory of a winner. Even Steve Jobs held one share of Apple (NASDAQ: AAPL) after he got fired. Remain connected to your investments for life.

5) **Make a strong case and track your results.** In our style of investing, the burden of proof is on the seller. We **prefer to search for great companies to hold for very long periods of time.** These sell rules don't work well for penny stocks or investments in speculative or promotional companies. Heck, we say sell those

off right now. But when you're in the zone of enduringly great companies, you owe it to yourself to thoroughly articulate why you are selling and, in the years after that sale, to track if that was the right decision. Never forget that **the long-term view is the most beautiful of all**.

QUICK SUMMARY

- **Buying and holding** trumps trading in the long run.
- There are certain circumstances when **selling makes sense**. These circumstances are either **specific to you**, the investor, or **the stock itself**.
- If you have to sell, **use extreme caution and follow the rules** outlined in this chapter.

CHAPTER 24

WHY DO WE NEVER INVEST WITH LEVERAGE?

Let me share an instructive lesson that I personally experienced just be-fore I started investing. That incident left such a deep impression, and by sharing the learnings that I took away with you, I hope you never have to experience it with your own capital and hard-earned money.

I had participated in a real-life "Investing Game" where we had five stocks to choose from. One could buy up to 20 times leverage (meaning you could use $1 to buy up to $20 worth of stocks). This was in a classroom setting with a total of 100 participants. There were 10-15 rounds depending on how the game went, and the goal was to have the largest portfolio by the end. Everyone contributed $50 each, and the winner with the largest portfolio value at the end of the game stood to win a cash prize of $2500.

In the first round, I was one of the few who went all in and took the maximum leverage possible to go long on all the stocks in equal weights of 20% each. The market went up 5% across all the stocks, and I doubled my original capital. The game host came around to interview me, and used words like "You are such a good investor right now, No. 1 in the first round, do you have any tips for the rest of the participants?" I remembered giving some cocky comments. And damn was I feeling pretty good and confident about myself. I was sure if I kept doing the same, I would be rocking this game.

In the second round, again the market climbed up 3%, and more people joined me in leveraging their portfolios to buy these stocks. I was feeling like I was at the top of the world, and I could see how everyone was envying me. Again, the game host interviewed me and asked me if I was going to sell any or go all in. I said I will keep holding all the stocks.

In the third round, there was a crisis and the market plunged 50%. My portfolio went to zero and **I was wiped out immediately by leverage.** About 70% of the participants in the class went along with me. I was feeling very emotional and upset.

The game continued with the market and up and down, and eventually, there were a handful of winners. They had either employed little leverage or were "lucky" to buy and sell right at the highs and lows with a few more cycles after that. The winner was one who employed little leverage at the beginning but realized never to use it after the third round and happened to buy and sell in partials throughout the game.

This lesson was extremely instructive for me:

1) **Never use leverage to borrow to invest in equities especially for the long-term,** regardless of what any financial media tells you— at least for the type of investing that we are doing or should be doing. If you are trading, it is a different thing altogether. Because of the short-term volatility of the down moves, which can be much larger than up moves, it can wipe you out at any time.

2) **When we invest, it is about staying in the game.** Only if you are in the game can you continue to compound your returns year after year. If you are out of the game, there's nothing you can do.

3) In games and in life, **you don't have to win to learn a lesson.** In fact, **when you lose, you learn even more**. I was grateful to have lost, got over it, and took away these precious learnings. I would

WHY DO WE NEVER INVEST WITH LEVERAGE?

rather lose in this game with no money involved than to actually
lose it during my actual investing.

4) **It was instructive as to how hard it was to time the market.** In
subsequent rounds, they allowed shorting and more participants
got taken out because they timed their shorts wrong and the
market purposely chopped around. Markets clearly can be more
irrational longer than you can remain solvent.

5) **Never be overconfident, always be humble.** You never know
what will happen. You can be No. 1 one day and be the last the
next day. Always be thinking forward, learning, and figuring out
what's next.

My biggest single takeaway is summarized by Warren Buffett below:

> *"I've seen **more people fail because of** liquor and **leverage** –
> leverage being borrowed money. **You really
> don't need leverage** in this world.
> **If you're smart, you're going to make a lot
> of money without borrowing**."*
> – *Warren Buffett*

Never borrow with leverage on margin to invest in equities. The volatility of the up and down moves can and will eventually wipe you out.
Markets will always be irrational longer than you can remain solvent.
I hope my personal story has allowed you to appreciate why we **do not
employ leverage** and advise against leverage when it comes to investing.

QUICK SUMMARY

- Winners in the stock market are those who **don't use leverage**,
  especially for the long-term.
- **Never borrow with leverage on margin to invest in equities.**
  The volatility of the up and down moves can and will eventually
  wipe you out.

CHAPTER 25

HOW DO WE INVEST AND ALLOCATE OUR CAPITAL?

The Rule of Buying in Thirds

If you want to invest in a company that you want to own, you can always buy a little first. You **can always buy in thirds**. That way if the **price goes up**, you would have **at least invested in some**, and add the second third then. And if the **price went down**, you should be **happy to add the second third at even lower prices than before and add more stocks**. You should only add the last third if the company has "proven its mettle" with higher prices over some time.

What we are trying to do here is **prevent and avoid regret minimization** and because remember **we do not know where the market will go next in the short-term but we know where it will go over the long run for great companies**. If you were waiting to buy at lower prices but the price kept moving higher, you ended up missing the boat. But if you have bought and the price moved lower, you still get another chance of adding to your position. Remember, you will end up with more stocks at lower prices (same dollar amount divided by lower stock price = more stocks), so the dollar cost averaging effect will be better.

Portfolio Allocation

For a person starting a new investment portfolio, this is how one can look to invest. Feel free to adjust it depending on your conviction. You can follow a similar framework even if you are an existing investor.

Let's assume we have $1 million to invest for the next 10-20 years, with an additional $50,000 to add every year. Let's look at the existing capital first. You can scale the numbers accordingly depending on what you have. But note this is a rough guideline.

We will split the $1 million into three increments of $300,000 (30% each x 3 totaling $900,000 to be made roughly every 6 months, keeping $100,000 remaining in cash for big market sell-offs to add to your highest conviction companies. Most important is to get some skin in the game as quickly as you can.

First Investment Round:

- Find **20-40 stocks**[56] that you would like to invest in. These should be some of your highest conviction ideas. If you don't have 40, start with 5, 10, but make it an even smaller part of your portfolio.
- **Start with equal weights in dollar amounts.**
- We're starting with equal weights to make your allocation decision simple and to help you get some exposure to each of our stocks.

Subsequent Three Investment Rounds (6 months later):

- **Identify 15-30 stocks** that you would like to **allocate more capital to** and increase your positions in subsequent second and third investment rounds, 6 months after.
- These can be (1) either from **existing higher conviction ideas** that are already doing well or (2) **adding a few new ideas**.

---

[56] If you don't have 40 companies, try to at least start with 20 and gradually add over time.

- Companies not living up to your expectations (business or financial performance declining worse than expected) should not be earning more of our capital.
- **Continue with equal weights.**

Remaining $100,000 and Subsequent $50,000 to Be Allocated Each Year

We will **keep the remaining $100,000 and subsequent $50,000 in cash** to take advantage of any market sell-offs within the year to add to existing positions or add new companies as starter positions that might not be ready for a full position in our portfolio.

As we get to know more about the business and the leadership team and gain better clarity on their market-beating potential, we'll invest more and "graduate" these to full positions.

For the new positions, try **investing small amounts into these stocks at first** and **building your position over time as they prove themselves.** Think of these as research positions that are all about getting some skin in the game, learning about these businesses, and allocating our capital accordingly.

Investing is about staying fully invested as much as possible, but we recognize the psychological importance of having some but not significant ammunition on the sidelines. **Stay flexible on when, what, and how much you want to add.**

Allocation on the Types of Companies

Also depending on where you are in your life, you can look at the following guidance and allocate the sector guidance accordingly (total should be 100%). If you are less than 10 years away from retirement and prefer more safety in your investments, you can shift much more titans (including Dividend Aristocrats) and proven winners. If you are younger or just starting out your career, you might want to have a higher allocation towards proven winners, emerging stars, and moonshots. **Key is to start wherever you are comfortable and learn along the way.**

Types of Companies	Portfolio Allocation (%)
Titans of the Industry	30-50%
Proven Winners	20-30%
Emerging Stars	15-25%
Moonshots	10-20%

When you invest long enough, you **will have some underperforming companies** (max -100%) from time to time. **It is okay.** Formerly great companies lose their edge all the time; it's a tenet of capitalism. Ultimately, the reason we invest in a wide range of companies is that some won't work out, and they will become a smaller and smaller percentage of our net worth. The **losers will end up becoming more insignificant and irrelevant with time.** If **we invest well,** the **gains from the winners**, especially the multibaggers (>>100%) **will far outweigh the inevitable losers** (max -100%). This is the game of investing that we will play, one that has the **odds skewed in our favor** (not stacked against us!) that Wall Street and very few do.

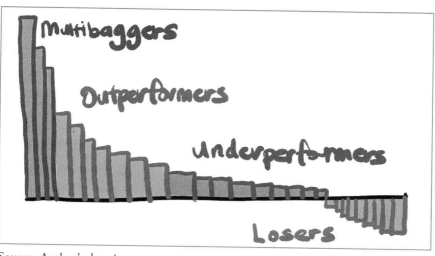

Source: Author's drawings

QUICK SUMMARY

- Buy a little of a stock at first by **buying in thirds**.
- **Find 20-40 stocks** you would like to invest in and invest an equal amount in each.
- In 6 months, **identify 15-30 stocks** you would like to put more capital into.
- Take **advantage of market sell-offs and new companies** by keeping capital aside to invest in these yearly.

CHAPTER 26

FINAL WORDS AND CONCLUDING REMARKS

These are the six traits of my investment framework summed up to invest in companies that are (1) Stalwarts leading the way, (2) Proven winners shaping our future and (3) Highfliers of the future that are becoming emerging stars or are still moonshots.

1) **Growth**: Revenues that are small in relation to a large and/or growing market, or revenues that are large in a fast-growing market. (Tailwinds, TAM, Revenue Growth, Market Share, Top Dog, Disruptors)

2) **Competitive Advantage:** Strong and improving sustainable competitive advantage resulting in revenue streams that are recurring in nature, either through contracts, business models, or customer behavior.

3) **Innovation**: A proven ability to grow, innovate, and continue to gain market share into the future.

4) **Profitability**: Strong and/or improving profitability with operating leverage, high likelihood of generating strong and growing streams of earnings, and free cash flows in the future.

5) **Financials**: Strong balance sheet with preferably net cash with little to no net debt.

6) **Management**: Founder-led and owned or solid management team with preferably high insider ownership with integrity, capability, and an innovative mindset.

7) **Vision**: Companies that are changing the world, innovating, solving new problems, and providing goods and services that are making our lives and the world a better place than before.

This book is a culmination of my investing journey in my quest and search to learn from the greatest and the best investors. David and Tom Gardner from The Motley Fool played a significant part in shaping how I invest. David Gardner certainly does not know me yet (hopefully I will get to meet him in person one day), but I have met Tom Gardner twice, once in Singapore and once in Washington, where Fool HQ is.

This was truly something that made the most sense to me: **Investing ultimately is a game that can be beaten**, and there are many approaches to take a swing at it. Value Investing is one. My way of Vision Investing is the other. I have combined all that I have learned from over five years and more than three years of actual investing.

What I have done is **demystify** and **use the truth to guide you on best practices for investing,** and I am sure both yours and our investing approach will continue to improve and change throughout our investing journey for the better.

Investing outperformance can be broken down into two simple factors: (1) **increasing the probability of you finding winning companies that will outperform the market consistently over the long term** and (2)

increasing your payoffs by investing, holding, and adding to these winners over the long term.

We have shared a number of U.S. companies as examples. Ultimately this book and its broad-based principles are meant for any investor out there wherever you are and can be applied in your country.

When you truly find and invest in companies that will outperform the market and have the **right mindset and psychology** to know especially how to react to market sell-offs, you are well primed to start your investing journey.

Always remember why we **only focus on the long-term** when it comes to investing: the likelihood of losing money is almost zero. More importantly, understand that the market truly is a **voting machine in the short-term** full of noise, **long-term it is a weighing machine,** and the best companies will eventually be rewarded.

Seek to invest in businesses with strong balance sheets, sustainable competitive advantages, talented and trustworthy leadership, and pricing power. As David Gardner rightly puts it, "**Find excellence, invest in excellence, and hold excellence**." Try investing this way instead, you might come to love it, and eventually be rewarded by it.

CHAPTER 27

SUMMARY OF COMMITMENTS

Commitment No. 1

We will not market time or trade with respect to our long-term investments.

Commitment No. 2

We commit and know we can invest better and beat the market.

Commitment No. 3

When we invest, we invest only for the long-term. Our holding period is forever.

Commitment No. 4

We understand that stocks will always go down faster than they go up, but stocks will go up more than they go down over time. Market sell-offs present buying opportunities for us, not selling opportunities.

Commitment No. 5

We commit to find and invest in the best companies for the long-term.

Commitment No. 6

We commit to understanding that the massive gains from a few of our multibagger winners, will more than offset the combined losses from our losers as they become negligible over time.

Commitment No. 7

We commit to have a diversified portfolio and own at least 15-25 stocks.

Commitment No. 8

We commit to reduce my borrowings where possible, be disciplined in our spending, save, and invest as much as we possibly can.

Commitment No. 9

We love companies with growing revenues and profits.

Commitment No. 10

We love companies that especially have operating leverage.

Commitment No. 11

We love companies that are financially strong and preferably have net cash.

Commitment No. 12

We love companies with growing revenues, profits, and cash flows.

Commitment No. 13

We especially love companies with negative CCC that get paid to do business.

Commitment No. 14

We commit to finding excellence, buying excellence, and adding to excellence over time. We sell mediocrity. That's how we invest.

Commitment No. 15

We almost never invest in turnaround companies.

Commitment No. 16

We prefer to own businesses that are founder-led and owned that have a good track record of running the business.

Commitment No. 17

We look for businesses that have moats, especially if they have multiple moats, making their moats wider. We especially love businesses that have network effects.

Commitment No. 18

We love strong businesses that are growing, have strong tailwinds in growing markets, and are growing their market share.

EXERCISE: WRITING YOUR OWN PREMISE, VISION, PURPOSE, STRATEGY

(1) My Premise - Investing

What are the new foundational beliefs you now hold? Are they empowering or disempowering? Do they move you at a deep level or are they holding you back? What is your premise for this area of your life?

_____

_____

_____

_____

_____

_____

_____

_____

Your Vision - Investing

Your vision refers to the ideal state you would like to achieve with respect to Investing. Ask yourself, how do you want your investments to do? What do you want to be doing on a consistent basis?

_____

_____

_____

_____

_____

_____

Your Purpose - Investing

Your purpose is your WHY. Why do you want to invest? Why do you want to do well in investing? What energizes you? What empowers you? What motivates you to achieve your vision? Describe your WHY. Go deep and ask yourself. Don't make it all only about money.

_____

_____

_____

_____

_____

_____

Your Strategy - Investing

Your strategy is your HOW and WHAT. Your strategy refers to the specific actions that will get you from where you are now to where you want to be. How will you bring your vision into reality? Ask yourself what kind of positive habits, attitudes, and actions steps you can implement. What is the strategy for the vision you want to create? Combine it with the winning principles you have learned, find what you think works for you, and discard those that you think otherwise.

_____

_____

_____

_____

_____

_____

_____

_____

GLOSSARY OF FINANCE TERMS[57]

Annual returns- The return that an investment provides over a period of time, expressed as a time-weighted annual percentage. Sources of returns can include dividends, returns of capital, and capital appreciation.

Asset- An asset is a resource with economic value that an individual, corporation, or country owns or controls with the expectation that it will provide a future benefit.

Bonds- A bond is a fixed income instrument that represents a loan made by an investor to a borrower (typically corporate or governmental).

Buy and hold- Buy and hold is a passive investment strategy in which an investor buys stocks (or other types of securities such as ETFs) and holds them for a long period regardless of fluctuations in the market.

Cash conversion cycle- The cash conversion cycle (CCC) is a metric that expresses the time (measured in days) it takes for a company to convert its investments in inventory and other resources into cash flows from sales.

Compound interest- Interest calculated on the initial principal, which also includes all of the accumulated interest from previous periods on a deposit or loan.

Cyclicals- A stock that's price is affected by macroeconomic or systematic changes in the overall economy.

---

[57] Source: Investopedia Dictionary
https://www.investopedia.com/financial-term-dictionary-4769738

ETFs- An exchange-traded fund (ETF) is a basket of securities that trade on an exchange, just like a stock.

Index funds- An index fund is a type of mutual fund or exchange-traded fund (ETF) with a portfolio constructed to match or track the components of a financial market index, such as the Standard & Poor's 500 Index (S&P 500).

Intraday- Intraday means "within the day." In the financial world, the term is shorthand used to describe securities that trade on the markets during regular business hours.

Investor- An investor is any person or other entity (such as a firm or mutual fund) who commits capital with the expectation of receiving financial returns.

Market price- The market price is the current price at which an asset or service can be bought or sold.

Multibaggers- A multibagger is an investment that has gained several times its original value.

Mutual fund- A mutual fund is a type of financial vehicle made up of a pool of money collected from many investors to invest in securities like stocks, bonds, money market instruments, and other assets.

P/E Ratio- The price-to-earnings ratio (P/E ratio) is the ratio for valuing a company that measures its current share price relative to its per-share earnings (EPS).

S&P 500- The S&P 500 or Standard & Poor's 500 Index is a market-capitalization-weighted index of the 500 largest U.S. publicly traded companies.

Sell-offs- A sell-off occurs when a large volume of securities is sold in a short period of time. Due to the law of supply and demand, this causes a corresponding decline in the price of the security.

Stocks- A stock (also known as equity) is a security that represents the ownership of a fraction of a corporation. This entitles the owner of the stock to a proportion of the corporation's assets and profits equal to how much stock they own.

Trader- A trader is an individual who engages in the buying and selling of financial assets in any financial market, either for himself or on behalf of another person or institution.

Unit trust- A unit trust is an unincorporated mutual fund structure that allows funds to hold assets and provide profits that go straight to individual unit owners instead of reinvesting them back into the fund.

ACKNOWLEDGMENTS

This book would have never been made possible without my wife and mother, who were there by my side to bring me back to recovery when I had my broken neck injury more than seven years ago. My wife has been a key supporter of my personal development and growth, and she was instrumental in pushing me to do more and become more.

Thank you, God, for granting me the opportunity to continue to live my life. I am thoroughly blessed and appreciative and strive to become better to be able to give back to the world.

It was T. Harv Eker's book *Secrets of the Millionaire Mind* that sparked a revolutionary change of my mindset and psychology, and how I should think about life and meaning. It was at his course "Mission to Millions" as part of the Quantum Leap personal development training that I discovered my life mission.

In my quest to learn to invest, I attended the Millionaire Investor Program (MIP) Value Investing program in Singapore. Ken Chee and his team at 8i combining lots of Warren Buffett's Value Investing teachings were instrumental to how I think about investing, specifically my mindset and my psychology. But what was more perceptive to me, was that while Value Investing appealed to me, I felt something was missing.

My quest to find other investing greats led me to The Motley Fool, specifically Tom and David Gardner and his team. I was perplexed by how foolproof their investing was and how they could beat the market consistently over the long run. They truly played a large part in influencing how

I invest. I joined the Motley Fool's Fool One membership, and ever since then, I became a regular weekly listener of David Gardner's Rule Breaker Investing Podcast (available on Spotify or iTunes) where he shares his insights into today's most innovative and disruptive publicly traded companies and how to profit from them. The Motley Fool truly are making the world smarter, happier, and richer. I was also recently deeply influenced by Peter Lynch and his book, *One Up on Wall Street* which features very similar thinking to how I invest.

Acknowledgments to my mentor, Diana Blanco and my Guerilla Business Initiative (GBI) trainer, Alex Mandossian for guiding me on my next step and to write this book, which I did in three weeks on a one-month gardening leave.

Final acknowledgments to my dearest friends, Chiam Ming Hwee, Raymond Heng, and Tham Zhi Yang, who kindly helped me review the book and provided the much-needed tips and structure. Final thanks to Rae Rashad, M.Ed. for helping with the final edits, Oyekola Sodiq Ajibola with the book cover design and Jose Pepito Jr. with the final formatting for publishing. I would not have been able to do it without all of your dedication, expertise and support.

ABOUT THE AUTHOR

Eugene Ng is the Founder and Chief Investment Officer of Vision Capital. Vision Capital manages only family funds and focuses on investing only in companies that reflect our best vision for our future. Vision Capital is a 100% long-only equity fund that does not employ leverage, short-selling, FX hedging, or the use of any derivatives or options to enhance portfolio returns. Vision Capital was first incepted on March 24, 2017, and the fund has outperformed the S&P 500 consecutively every year since. Vision Capital has since returned 143.0% compared to 30.1% for the S&P 500, with returns in excess of 112.9%[58].

Born and raised in Singapore, Eugene studied economics and finance where he received his Summa Cum Laude from the Singapore Management University in 2008. Eugene is also a keen sportsman, and he represented the Singapore National Team in Water Polo in the 2007 South East Asia (SEA) Games where they won their 22nd consecutive Gold.

Eugene's career in finance spans over 11 years. His career started in 2008, joining Citi as a management associate for 3 years. Subsequently, he moved to J.P. Morgan to do FX and interest rates institutional sales, covering corporations for over 8 years where he was a Vice-President.

To find out more about Vision Capital, visit visioncapital.group

---

[58] Source: Author's unaudited broker statements for the period 24 March 2017 – 30 June 2020

Printed in Poland
by Amazon Fulfillment
Poland Sp. z o.o., Wrocław

62143565R00193